Buses
ANNUAL

Edited by Gavin Booth

LONDON

IAN ALLAN LTD

Acknowledgements

The photographs in this year's *Buses Annual* were supplied by:

John Aldridge 124, 125, 126 (lower), 127-129
G. H. F. Atkins 16-20
P. M. Battersby 53 (top)
Gavin Booth Cover, 47 (lower), 48, 54-59, 92, 121-123
Gavin Booth Collection 21 (centre)
Stewart J. Brown 94-100, 126 (upper)
G. Coxon 22-28, 90/91, 104 (upper)
Alan B. Cross 83, 85
Michael Dryhurst 86, 88, 89
Michael Dryhurst Collection 80
M. Fowler 103, 104 (lower)
D. Fereday Glenn 117-120
Robert E. Jowitt 53 (bottom), 71-75, 93 (upper)
David Kaye 101
Charles F. Klapper 111, 115
Charles F. Klapper Collection 113
Iain MacGregor 47 (upper)
Robert F. Mack 36-39
G. R. Mills 105 (bottom), 106-110
T. W. Moore Endpapers, 30-35
Don Morris 41, 76-79, 105 (top)
A. Moyes 5, 7, 9, 10, 21 (bottom), 29
John Parke 65, 66, 68
Martin J. Perry 49-52
Jasper Pettie 40
R. H. G. Simpson 8, 37 (upper)
Viewfinder 11-15, 21 (top left/right), 60-64, 93 (lower)
R. L. Wilson 42-46, 53 (centre), 67, 69, 70, 105 (centre)

First published 1978

ISBN 0 7110 0862 0

Published by Ian Allan Ltd, Shepperton, Surrey, and printed in the United Kingdom by Ian Allan Printing Ltd

Contents

What are they looking at?

See page 21

See page 53

See page 93

Introduction

Two of the less glamorous aspects of the business are featured in this year's *Buses Annual*. There is a look at buses on special works services, by A. Moyes, and a T. W. Moore photo-essay on school buses in Warwickshire. But the leisure market is not forgotten, and there are articles on the attractions of seaside buses, and G. Coxon describes transport in and around Scarborough.

The vehicles themselves are covered in several features. The way they look is examined in Ray Stenning's admiring analysis of Duple's Commander range of coach bodies, and there is a photo-feature on the service bus bodies produced by Plaxton, a name more readily identified with luxury coachwork. One aspect of bus design which is often forgotten, and rarely illustrated in books like this, is the back end, so D. Fereday Glenn rectifies this omission in a photo-feature.

The wide acceptance of underfloor and rear-engines has caused a steady drop in the number of half-cab buses on the road; Robert E. Jowitt pays homage to a layout considered to be traditionally British.

The varied buses operated by Western SMT are described by Jasper Pettie, and Michael Dryhurst recalls the buses that have passed his various front doors. There are photo-features on second-hand trolleybuses, and on East Anglian buses which have served different operators. And looking at the bus in a wider sense, John Aldridge asks if the European bus is myth or reality.

The widely different places where buses work are covered by articles and photo-features. Martin J. Perry writes of the Teme Valley, and the independent operators which service that part of the country bordering England and Wales; John Parke recalls almost 37 years of personal acquaintance with Irish buses; David Kaye describes bus services on Humberside. And there are photo-features on Lincolnshire, Somerset and Paisley, and a look at municipal buses in the 1950s.

The other main articles are by Charles F. Klapper, looking back at interchange schemes in the London area, and Stewart J. Brown, investigating the case of the missing municipalities. The remaining photo-features gather together a light-hearted selection of odd photographs of buses — and, indeed, photographs of odd buses.

If the *Annual* contents sound mixed, that is the intention. I hope they are sufficiently mixed to suit the varied tastes of *Annual* readers.

Gavin Booth
Edinburgh

A Cynon Valley AEC Reliance/Willowbrook at Tower Colliery, Hirwaun.

Journeys to Work

A. MOYES takes a look at buses in their most utilitarian sense — the often unsung and unseen buses which provide special journeys for workers throughout Britain.

At the time of the 1971 Census, some five million journeys were made to work per day by bus in England and Wales alone. These accounted for only one-third of the work journeys made by all means other than walking, but they strongly affected the character of the bus industry. Without the journey-to-work, traffic peaks would be less; fleets would not need to contain that characteristic tail-end of low-mileage vehicles — often the old, the unusual, the difficult-to-drive or -maintain, and the most interesting to the enthusiast. But it also provides other fields of interest.

Bus networks serve a multitude of functions, and journeys-to-work are often catered for by regular interval services meeting a variety of needs. But surely only a worker or an enthusiast would be travelling on the regular interval services plying as early as 04.25 in west Cumbria, or between Immingham and Grimsby at 02.48. Perhaps those activities which do not fit within the normal transport structure are of most interest — the rush-hour duplicates and short

workings, contract buses, and non-psvs. Since facilities are often being provided for a limited and knowledgeable clientele, information about routes, vehicles and timings can be difficult to unearth. The larger stage carriage operators can be secretive about their rush-hour commitments, and though some contract services can be found in *Notices and Proceedings*, diligent research can be required.

The need for special facilities for workers' travel depends partly on the location of workplaces. Public transport tends to focus strongly on town or city centres, so that these are the most accessible points to most people. Cross-town or circumferential journeys may be more difficult, so that suburban employers are much less accessible by public transport, unless tailor-made facilities are provided — for a minimum worthwhile number of workers. Works buses are often required to cope with shift workers' times of travel; similarly, the flurries of Eastern Scottish lunchtime extras in the Borders woollen towns of Hawick and Galashiels hurrying the working wives home and back to work represent another type of unusually-peaked travel demand.

Works travel is often associated, therefore, with large-scale, out-of-town-centre employment, ranging from isolated mines and quarries, to major building sites (such as nuclear power stations both during and after construction), suburban factories or office complexes. The London New Towns provide clear examples of deliberate clustering of employment away from town centres, and have evoked the response of express works buses from industrial to housing areas in Stevenage in particular. Special buses are often needed where a factory has moved to a suburban location but still recruits staff from the former area. Possibly one of the earliest works buses was a mammoth 104-seater AEC which the company ran to the new AEC factory at Southall in 1927, from the former factory at Walthamstow. In tram days, equivalent facilities were unusual, though the Belfast shipyards justified a spur, and the Trafford Park industrial estate in Manchester an internal network; at Huddersfield and Rotherham, special trolleybus branches were similarly provided for rush-hour extras to the ICI works at Deighton and Silverwood colliery respectively.

Some of the appeal of works buses arises from their routes and termini. Though aesthetics are personal, industry can provide some of the most dramatic scenic backcloths for the bus photographer. Pithead gear at collieries can be particularly effective, though like some other concerns, the Coal Board does not encourage unauthorised photography on its premises, and some of its newer pitheads, such as Bold colliery, are rather anaemic. Steelworks can be stimulating, though buses can be dwarfed by the silhouettes of blast furnaces and rolling mills. Some steel works require internal transport, as at Llanwern, where Newport Corporation's Metro-Scanias cruise around in a rust-red haze. Unfortunately, many industrial activities are conducted in more nondescript buildings. The black corrugated iron shops beloved of World War 2 premises like Royal Ordnance Factories provide a gloomy, bland backdrop, useful for light-coloured vehicles. Some of these premises, characteristically built in remote spots for security reasons, remain interesting spots for the bus enthusiast, like the Glascoed one near Pontypool, though now requiring nothing like the 200-or-so vehicles once needed.

Terminal arrangements at works vary considerably. In the 1950s, quite sophisticated bus stations were built at some large factories; the Ferodo brake-linings firm was particularly proud of its efforts at its Chapel-en-le-Frith factory in Derbyshire, where up to 40 buses would congregate at the attractively-landscaped stands at peak hours. Unfortunately, with increasing use of cars for journeys to work, such facilities have often been partly or wholly demoted to car parks since. Sophisticated in a different way is the spur of the Runcorn busway which serves the Whitehouse industrial estate. With its bus-activated traffic lights like railway signals, it gives the uncanny impression of a narrow gauge railway formation on which someone has forgotten to lay tracks. Conversely, the terminal at the entrance to the Port Talbot steelworks must surely be the most vandalised and bleak spot ever graced by buses. Most works buses merely drop their loads at convenient spots on a site, often a clocking-in office, but for savagery, the destination of Messrs Dew's vehicles must take some beating. This Oldham contractor has a quarry overlooking the upper Tame valley about 1100 feet above sea level, to which a fleet of secondhand Bristol L-type single-deckers used to heave up a punishing, spiralling unmade track, to the quarry face. Here, the Bristols would be left for the day among the excavators, the crushers and the mud. Access roads to industrial sites can also be photogenic, such as the mile-long private road leading down to sylvan Pleasley Vale Mills near Mansfield. Indeed, works buses can be associated with several secretive places, as with some timetabled journeys on Crosville's route G2 at Wrexham, which penetrate the security fence at the Celanese factory which is otherwise closed to the public.

Works buses could first be searched for in public timetables, but operators show a variety of approaches to disclosure. Some conceal all such services, maybe stating that works buses run when required and are therefore liable to alteration or cancellation. Timetable policy depends partly on whether such facilities have separate Commissioners' licences; if not, they are often incorporated within ordinary timetables where they can provide welcome variety compared with often visually-repetitive regular-interval services. Symbols lead the eye to footnotes which can vary from the staccato to the lyrical, the esoteric to the explicit. There is nothing particularly gripping about Greater Manchester's Wigan area timetable offering 'additional journey 16.35 Heinz Factory to Wigan' though its '17.38 Old Engine to Depot' is better. However, who could resist a passage in a former Red & White timetable about an early morning gem in Ebbw Vale, an 06.10 from the Palace via Eureka to Hot Mill and Cold Mill?

Some operators segregate works extras at the back of their timetables, though quite a few, like South Wales Transport, PMT and Yorkshire Traction, ignore coal miners' services entirely. Perhaps SWT feel that the publicity at collieries is better than any timetable — at Abernant colliery near Ammanford, a huge notice at the bus park exhorts: 'no night shift buses to leave this yard until 06.50' in admonitory capitals. In contrast, timetables of operators like Ribble, East Midland, Barton, Trent and Hants & Dorset have seemingly comprehensive appendices for works (and school) extras. Others sprinkle them within the main text. Quite unique must be Crosville's faithful bilingualism in its western area timetable, which

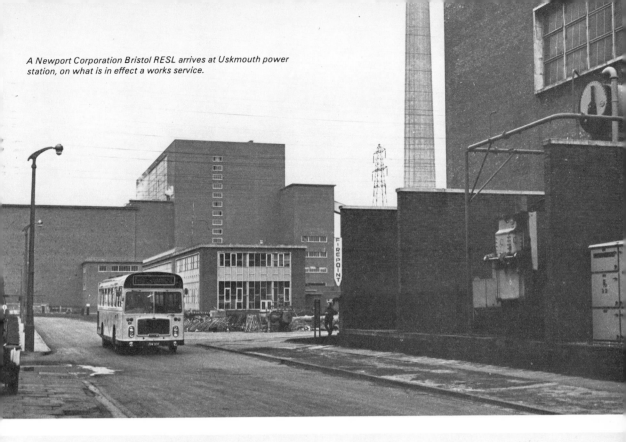

A Newport Corporation Bristol RESL arrives at Uskmouth power station, on what is in effect a works service.

Against an undistinguished National Coal Board background, Wigan Corporation Leyland Titan PD2s at Bold Colliery near St Helens in February 1963.

One of five AEC Regent V/Park Royal bought new in the early 1960s by the Atomic Energy Research Establishment at Harwell, Berks, for workers transport.

Right: *Bound for the well-known Latin quarter of Anglesey? This Crosville Bristol Lodekka FSF6B is, in fact, making ready for a trip to the aluminium smelter of Rio Tinto at Holyhead, from Amlwch depot.*

laboriously translates such destinations as 'Point of Ayr Colliery' near Holywell into the vernacular 'Glodfa'n Parlwr Du'.

Equally variable are operators' practices of identifying vehicles on works services. London Transport and London Country are predictably fastidious, giving such researchers as Barry Kosky plenty of recording to do. Many others sink to the general 'Private', 'Duplicate', 'Works Service' or 'Colliery Bus'. But even purpose-designed abbreviations can be as perplexing to the uninitiated. A regular North Western sight in Stockport's Mersey Square in the 1950s was an evening timing on route 75 displaying '61 M.U.' (ie Maintenance Unit No 61 at Woodford). Crosville loved abbreviations on their blinds some years ago; at times, Wrexham was full of tired Bristols labelled 'W.I.E.' (Wrexham Industrial Estate). But now they are almost exemplary in this respect, with specific displays like 'Celanese' or 'Bowaters'. Where second-hand species end up with contractors and retain their former blinds, the way is open for waggish drivers to express their sense of

humour. An ex-Thames Valley Bristol LL6B saloon with Precelly, of Clynderwen, used to ply to the Royal Aircraft Establishment at Aberporth near Cardigan with its full set of High Wycombe blinds showing 'Sands: Local Service'; an ex-Merseyside (Wirral) Leyland Titan with Harrison Mayer of Stoke-on-Trent displays anything from Landican to Noctorum; and where three-track number blinds remain installed, the legend '007' is a monotonous favourite.

Perhaps the journey-to-work means most to the enthusiast because of vehicles used. A whole fleet's character may be conditioned by works needs. At Aberdare, for instance, the UDC's heavy commitment to colliery services and the rarity of pithead baths led it to specify slatted wooden seats until 1956, when it felt that the miners of Abergorki and Penrikyber were now sufficiently clean to merit moquette. At Stockport, the Corporation had to retain 20 Leyland TS7 and TS8 saloons, with interesting English Electric bodies, for specials to a group of large factories on Bird Hall Lane, Cheadle Heath. These lay stranded beyond a low railway bridge which could not accommodate

double-deckers until reconstructed in 1963. Only two single-deckers would otherwise have been needed, for the Corporation's other restricted route.

Operators living almost wholly on works services and contracts often favour varied, short-life fleets, with a rapid turnover of vehicles, creating difficulties but also fascination for the vehicle recorder. For non-psv operators of works services to buy new vehicles is rare enough to be interesting — at least, vehicles larger than, say, minibuses or the Leyland Redline. The United Kingdom Atomic Energy Authority's Harwell establishment began bus operation some 25 years ago with secondhand (mainly ex-London Transport) stock but soon graduated to new Bedford SB buses, then new AEC Renowns, which are, one hears, about to be replaced by three new Bristol VRT/ECW double-deckers. Unusually, a London maker of tobacco processing machines, Molins, bought a pair of all-Crossley sds of unique straight waistrail body style in 1950, which were good enough to pass six years later to a stage carriage independent near Wrexham; Molins then indulged in Bedford SBs with bodies — it

transpired after a lot of detective work in the pages of *Buses Illustrated* — by Owen.

When buying new, the non-psv operator can indulge in his own livery. Some national contractors have their own house-style; the bright yellow of Wimpey, or the grey favoured by McAlpines are often smarter these days than the unkempt NBC schemes. Often, however, vehicles passing into the hands of a works bus operator keep a previous livery. Perhaps Bedlington & District Coaches, in Northumberland, represents the most interesting repercussions of this, in buying City of Oxford AEC Regents in the late 1950s, and repainting its whole fleet into two reds and duck egg green. A few years later, ex-Southport Crossley and AEC double-deckers arrived, and inspired a mass repaint into Southport-style red and cream on to such oddities as ex-Maidstone & District Bristol K/Weymann, ex-Oxford AEC Regal/Willowbrook and ex-Thames Valley Bristol LL types. Large-scale operators of works services with double-deckers, such as Bedlington, Warners of Tewkesbury, or Ensign of Hornchurch, have often built up quite standardised fleets. But even here, an oddity can exist — the Warners' ex-demonstrator Dennis Loline with attractive Northern Counties bodywork, now clad in a swirling all-over advertisement for Warners' own garage, forms a welcome contrast with its fleet-mates' unrelieved green.

The smaller non-psv fleets may almost perversely contain no vehicle alike; a classic must be the builder Gittins of Johnstown near Wrexham, whose fleet in the early 1970s was a preservationists' delight, with a rare ex-Phillips, Holywell, Seddon, an ex-County, Lepton, Leyland PS1/Brush, and one of the Crossleys new to Molins, mentioned earlier. Long may such 'operators' remain, even if their passengers may not appreciate the vehicles' rarity as they trundle to their next building job.

The journey to work can, therefore, provide several distinct facets of interest for the transport student. Provision of works' transport is now changing its character; the accountants scrutinising the practices of the larger stage-carriage operators are perhaps causing operators to be less keen to undertake rush-hour commitments, if no off-peak work is available. If anything, for the employer, or the small operator with part-time staff, scope to undertake works transport has increased. Recent surveys in Hertfordshire suggest that works coaches provide for about 30 per cent of bus commuting in the county. Indeed, in Somerset, widening the availability of works buses to the general public forms an important part of the county's Transport Policy and Programme. The works bus sector seems likely, therefore, to maintain its interest for the enthusiast.

A Potteries Leyland Leopard/Marshall seen after bringing miners to the now-closed Norton Colliery, Stoke-on-Trent, from Milton in September 1975.

A COMMANDING LEAD

RAY STENNING

Coach design responds to fashion, but to succeed it has to meet certain parameters. A coach has to project a sense of purpose, an image of now, a feeling of security, an inviting aura, a little bit of — what can you call it — dash, spirit, élan, style? Whatever the word, it is just that very enigmatic indefinable quality, that trigger to set the adrenalin flowing, that 'it' that the Duple Commander in its final Mk IV form had!

Powerful ways to describe a mere coach body, but to my feeling for design there was a coach that summed up a whole philosophy of design thought — and what's more, it was human. I mean that one could (or at least, I could) relate to it. It had evolved, grown up, found its full flowering through development — *and* it had its faults (I did say it was human).

Later on to people's eyes it became out-moded — still striking and handsome but of a past season, last year's fashion, passé. Timeless elegance usually lacks that very excitement that is needed in modern coach design, and appeals to the purist more than the passengers. The paradox that it was both strikingly elegant and outrageously vulgar at the same time has ensured that it remains a classic.

Yes, the Commander may seem dated now, but none of its successful points has diminished except a feeling for the present — only the present has moved on. It did succeed on every count, including the added one that to reach a pinnacle in design or style involves knowing when you've reached it, knowing when to go no further, to change the scene. Such is the substance of legends!

How did the Commander develop, this legend occur? We need to go back to the early 1960s to trace the 'star's' rising. At that time Duple had recently launched a new range of body styles with a strong family resemblance. The Bella Vista for the Bedford VAS, Bella Vega for the SB (called Trooper when on the equivalent Ford chassis) and Vega Major for the new twin-steer Bedford VAL chassis. There was also the Commodore on the short AEC Reliance and Leyland Leopard chassis, but in contrast to the

An original Mk I Commander, still performing front rank service with National Travel a decade later. The simple elegance of that finely proportioned front was to be changed for something less attractive at the end of 1965.

enormous success of others, this version of the 'Bella' range failed to find a market.

It was the market that this model was aimed at, the 'big fleet' operators, that eluded Duple sales. They hadn't a suitable model with which to break into, for example, the BET fleets that had patronised their products in the past — a model for the heavyweight underfloor-engined chassis, the 36-footers that made up an increasing proportion of the big firms' express fleets. Production at Duple's Blackpool factory (as distinct from Hendon, home of the Bella range) included the Continental and its visually superior stablemate, the Alpine Continental, but in contrast to Harrington and Plaxton products, their popularity was slight.

To widen their market, Duple announced for the 1964 season, in July 1963, some additions to the range. A version of the Vega Major, the Marauder, was supplied on the new Ford Thames 36 chassis, but the twin sensations of the 1964 range were striking new designs for the underfloor-engined heavyweights, the Astrocoach and Commander. As with many designs,

the Astrocoach was built subject to enquiry, hence the one prototype, BTU 22B, remained the sole example of this advanced model, but the distinguishing feature of curved glass panels taking the window area up into the roof formed the basis of the later, highly successful though visually disastrous Viceroy range — the greenhouse-on-wheels one (greenhouse-on-casters if on a Bedford VAL)!!

The Plaxton Panorama was catching on fast in the big fleets and the Commander was Duple's counter-attack. Plaxton influence was its most noticeable feature for it sported a panoramic window treatment of flattering similarity. Perhaps less brutal than the Panorama, the Commander featured the familiar and finely-proportioned front with a graceful line and clean

11

This Hants & Dorset Leopard was formerly with Southdown. That front always looked rather sorry for itself and the all-white National livery makes it more prominent.

Right: *Maidstone & District turned to Duple for touring coaches when Harrington stopped production, and bought several batches. One of the first batch is seen here — a Mk III Commander. The M&D traditional livery was particularly unsuited to the angular lines of the body.*

profile that really did seem to have timeless elegance. Twelve years later some of these models were still performing front rank service for National Travel. The model soon found ready buyers in the market at which it was aimed — Midland Red, PMT, Black & White, for example. Some of the Black & White coaches were on the troublesome Daimler Roadliner chassis, for the drawing office produced designs suitable for various chassis. East Kent chose the Commander for some short AEC Reliance touring coaches, equally handsome at this length, such was the good design of the Commander.

The maxim 'familiarity breeds contempt' may have been the reasoning behind a new face worn by Duple models towards the end of 1965. Duple was producing a wide range of bodies along two distinct themes by then. The facelifted Bella range continued with variations to suit the new Bedford VAM and Ford R192 chassis, whilst Blackpool concentrated mainly on the Commander with its derivative for the VAM and R192, the Viscount.

The new front grafted on to the proven Commander lines was less than successful. It was a brave attempt to keep up to date and ahead of the opposition, and the idea behind the look could not be faulted — just its execution. Visually the idea was to throw more emphasis on the horizontal and in keeping with the sense of purpose add an

aggressive thrust-forward, forward-thinking, forward-looking image. Well, it did this all right, but gone was the classically-proportioned front, replaced by something that could at best be described as indiscriminate and ugly. Coarse and flashy — like American cars of yore (and now?) — the whole look was marred by crude details.

The heavily-hooded headlights were placed uncomfortably on a body line, immediately disrupting the sought-after horizontal emphasis. A cheap and nasty mesh grille in a heavy surround of unrelated shape was at loggerheads with the rest of the style. The eye had too many conflicting stimuli — in a word, disharmony. But it was a look, an

Hants & Dorset-owned from new, this is one of four Bristol RESH coaches — the only Mk II Commanders produced. Note the Viceroy influence with the peaked front and roof toplights to the windows. The straight waistline can be compared with the slight dip to the rear of the Mk I.

Right: *Southdown has often shown a disdain for brightwork. Plain panels were specified instead of stainless steel embellishment on some Panoramas and Commander Mk IV touring coaches. Southdown's individuality is also expressed in the inclusion of opening windows. This view visibly demonstrates the feeling of 'forward motion' with parallel lines and raked-forward front panels.*

individual look, a Duple look, and it is obvious with hindsight that it was simply part of the evolutionary process — its adolescence if you like.

I think it was obvious at the time that a cleaning-up would soon result, but not before the Commander in its later Mk I form found a few more converts — Southdown and North Western were just two of them. Neither would it come before a peculiar and rare Mk II model emanated from the Blackpool drawing office, coded FS63/31, and built for Hants & Dorset in 1967, their four examples being the total Mk II production.

The Viceroy, mentioned earlier, had meanwhile come on to the market, intended for lightweight chassis. The Mk II Commander was a strange amalgam of the Commander concept and Viceroy features. A straight waistline without the gentle dip to the rear previously employed, heralded future Commander styling, as did the prominent peak over the windscreen. The chief similarity to the Viceroy, however, was the hooked trim line, a direct copy, and the use of roof toplights.

Apart from the lack of co-ordination of the sourly-grinning front, it was a look that would soon date, as it did not even have an element of elegance with which to justify itself. In July 1967 something rather exciting came from Blackpool, the Mk III. One could now see the

model growing up. To all intents and purposes an entirely new model, it did bear a marvellous family resemblance — one could see its parentage, its pedigree, the evolution was obvious.

The straight waistline, forward-sloping front and rear screen pillars and deeper windows all contributed to the theme of horizontal motion. Here was a coach that really turned heads. What people noticed most was the definitive front end. The same theme was graphically expressed here, in no uncertain terms — the same theme that was attempted unsuccessfully in the later Mk I. Aggressiveness intimated by that front end had been replaced by a look of authority, of power, of

command. It was the same visual idea of a wide grille above the headlamp panel but squared up and refined. And it really did relate to the rest of the design. The grille, horizontally barred and slightly recessed in its sharp surround was taken to the extreme width, and its perfectly rectangular shape raked forward at just the right degree to stress the 'Commander' theme, as did the similarly raked peak over the screen. Just two elements spoiled the effect. One was the fussy headlight panel with its heavy bumper and the other was an uncomfortable step in the side trim.

A year later, in July 1968, the climax of Commander evolution was brought into production, displaying

the work of design consultant Carl Olsen. Simple, subtle changes to the Mk III transformed an already good-looking coach into one that was nothing short of striking. It really did express in metal form the concept of coaching. As for a sense of purpose — it looked as though it was going somewhere just standing still !

Finer bumpers with rubber inserts protected the corners and coupled with the new headlamp panel gave the front a lighter, cleaner look and integrated it visually with the side. The headlamps were recessed behind a toughened glass panel unobtrusively set in a stainless steel band, this horizontally ribbed band continuing unbroken the entire length of the bodyside to meet the rear lamp units at the same level. All other lower side trims were done away with.

Running the full length of the bodysides also, above the windows at cantrail level, was a matching stainless steel ribbed band. These two combined and the absense of any conflicting visual information (the untidy Mk III kicked line) enhanced the pure sense of horizontal motion. Every line, every surface, led the eye in that plane and

Compare the Mk III (left) and Mk IV (above). The unsatisfactory 'step' in the Mk III body line was replaced by a horizontal stainless steel band running the full length of the Mk IV bodyside, stressing forward motion. The bright panel added above the Mk IV windows continues the horizontal theme and makes the window area seem greater. The fussy headlamp panel and heavy bumper of the Mk III gave way to a tidier treatment on the Mk IV which relates the front to the side. The Mk IV front (right) represents Olsen's clean, tidy and harmonious solution to the Duple front.

Left: *In National livery, this Greenslades Reliance demonstrates the striking use of line and angle on the Mk IV Commander.*

the screen pillars, of physical and visual necessity thicker, being raked forward animated the line. A clever design 'trick' was that these elements, especially the side bands low down, reduced the apparent height of the bodyside thereby contributing to the sense of horizontal motion, which in turn helped reduce the height, which then . . . you get it ! I don't think any other designer has mastered the use of the straight line and sharp angles to such an uncannily emotive degree.

And that was about it. To try to update the look would have pushed it into a caricature. As the pinnacle had been reached, the Mk IV remained in production winning more converts to the style until 1970, by which time nearly 450 of all Marks had been built, and Duple wisely left well alone. It had had its glory and the fashion-conscious coach world would soon turn to something else. Whether that something else would meet the parameters of modern coach design is a matter for further debate. The Dominants, even in their tarted-up Michelotti guise, and the Plaxton Panorama Supremes have yet to set my adrenalin flowing at the same

dizzy rate. They don't command my senses. They haven't got 'it'.

Perhaps the Willowbrook Spacecar, in the hands of the right designer could develop into a head-turner — it's almost that already. I hope so, for the Commander needs a successor and the industry needs exciting coaches. They stimulate demand, they are its bait. I must thank Mr Studd of Duples for allowing me access to certain information, but mainly I must thank Duples themselves for having designed, built and developed the Commander, and their many customers for having bought it.

Lincs with the Past

Photographs by G. H. F. ATKINS

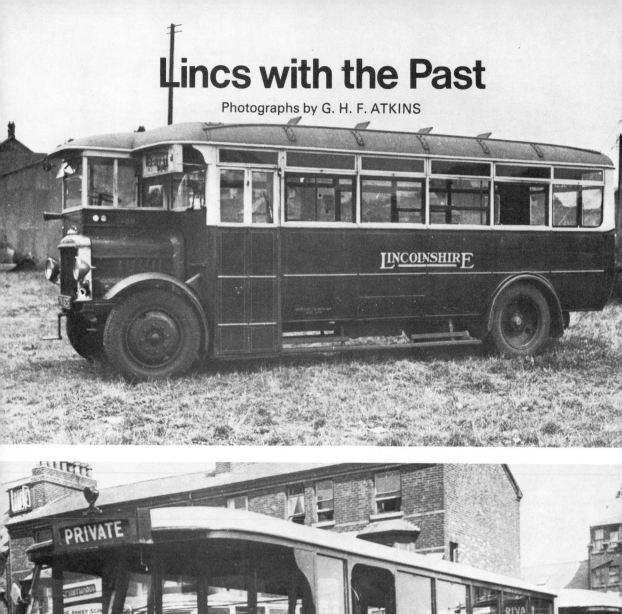

Left: *This Lincolnshire Road Car Co veteran was an ADC 415 acquired in 1931 from the fleet of United Automobile Services, then based at Lowestoft. United also built the 35-seat body. It is seen here in 1934.*

Above: *An early product of the so-called 'streamline era', a 1932 Lincolnshire Leyland Tiger TS4 with Lincoln-built Rainforth 30-seat coach body, seen at Skegness in 1939.*

Right: *At Grantham in 1935, a smart Leyland LT5A Lion, with metal construction Leyland 34-seat bus body.*

Left: *An older Leyland Lion, a PLSC model which passed to Lincolnshire from Retford Motor Services. Seen here in 1929, the bus body was by John Taylor, Barnsley.*

Right: *An elegant Leyland design of the mid-1930s, a 1936 Leyland Tiger TS7 with 34-seat Leyland body. The photograph, taken in 1936, clearly shows the prewar livery of dark and light green, with off-white window pillars and roof.*

When this Brighton Hove & District AEC
Regent was photographed in Lumley
Road, Skegness, in 1954, it was
operating on hire to Lincolnshire, but with
several of its brothers it was
subsequently bought. It was new in
1931, and had a 1944 ECW 56-seat
body.

One of the Leyland/Beadle rebuilds of the
early postwar period, this 1948
33-seater, seen in 1949 at the
Lincolnshire garage in Skegness, was
based on a 1934 Leyland Cub KP3.

A contrast in models from the
Bristol/ECW stables, at Nottingham in
1955. 2077 was a 1939 L5G with
32-seat rear entrance body, bought by
Lincolnshire from Eastern Counties in
1954; alongside is 2212, a then new
LS5G with 41-seat dual-purpose body.

Above: *Skegness in 1929, and a 1926 Vulcan toastrack of the grey-painted fleet of Tom Cary Ltd. It later passed into the Lincolnshire fleet.*

Below: *At the same bus stop in 1967, a 1954 Bristol LD6B with 58-seat ECW body.*

At Huntingdon Street, Grantham in 1954, ex-London Transport B11, which had passed to Lincolnshire in 1953. It was a 1945 Bristol K6A with Duple 56-seat body.

This very restricted bus station in High Street, Lincoln, was used for many years until the large new garage and bus station was opened in 1959. The bus here in 1958 was a 1946 AEC Regal I with 35-seat Duple body, bought in 1950 from Enterprise, Scunthorpe.

Curiouser and Curiouser/1

Greenslades 341 with misplaced passenger...

being watched in Taunton bus station.

This started out as an official photograph of a Dunfermline & District tramcar and brand-new Alexanders replacement bus, but something happened to the photographic plate. The tram was Dunfermline 26, and the bus was Alexanders R147, a 1937 all-Leyland Titan TD4.

A non-runner? This former Crosville 1946 Bristol L6A, converted to front entrance for one-man operation, was abandoned after it passed to Thomas (Silver Star), from Hughes-Jones. It is seen at Rhostryfan in 1975.

Scarborough Seaside Special

The buses that serve one of England's most popular seaside holiday resorts, and the coaches that bring tourists in their thousands, are described by G. COXON.

Scarborough is one of England's oldest holiday resorts and was once famous for its fashionable Spa; the water has now gone, but the Spa buildings are still to be seen along the sea front. Since the administrative boundaries were redrawn in 1974, Scarborough is now part of the county of North Yorkshire, and is surrounded by other new counties, Cleveland to the north, Humberside to the south, and West Yorkshire to the west.

Scarborough has two fine sandy beaches, the North Sands and the South Sands, which are separated by a rocky seagull-infested promontory on top of which stands the ruins of the 12th century castle. The town attracts over 1½ million visitors each year, the majority during the peak summer months of July and August, and proudly claims that it has something for everybody.

Tourism is Scarborough's main industry, although it does have a small harbour next to the South Sands where a small amount of cargo is handled and a number of fishing boats are based. Plaxton's of Scarborough, the well-known coachbuilder and building contractor, is one of the major industrial companies providing employment.

Although Scarborough has a borough council, it operates no buses of its own. It was in 1931 that the council made an agreement with United which permitted that company to operate the town services in return for one penny payable to the council for each mile involved. This unusual arrangement survived until early in 1978, when the special Town fares structure was dropped, and fares were charged on United's normal scale. As mileage information was needed for the council, the local United fleet was split into two, Scarborough Town and Scarborough Country, although the vehicles involved had no external differential features.

During 1977 most of United's buses there were fitted with new full-length blinds so that both Town and Country routes could be covered by the vehicles, thus allowing greater flexibility and providing a more detailed destination blind for the large influx of

Opposite: *A United Leyland National on a town service.*

Left: *United's Vernon Street depot with a Bristol LH/Plaxton coach and delightful plasterwork.*

holidaymakers. It was a common practice for most of the town service vehicles to display the route number, with the United fleetname in the destination box. United has one garage, in Vernon Street, which is close to the main bus station at Valley Bridge. This was originally United's own bus station, but since becoming part of the NBC, rationalisation has meant that the two other NBC operators with services to Scarborough, East Yorkshire and West Yorkshire, have moved to Valley Bridge as well.

During the peak season United has to acquire vehicles in order to cope with the extra summer-only schedules, and for a few years now batches of old vehicles from other NBC subsidiaries have added interest to the local scene. Approximately 74 vehicles are allocated to Scarborough during the summer, with the former Country fleet taking a slightly larger share than the Town fleet; included in the Country fleet were the summer season's acquisitions. During 1977 United acquired nine vehicles; they were two Leyland Leopard/Weymann 49-seat semi-coaches from neighbours East Yorkshire, one Leyland Leopard/Willowbrook 53-seat bus from East Midland, two Bristol LH6L/ECW 43-seat buses from Southern Vectis, and four Bristol/ECW 70-seat Lodekkas from East Midland — two FLF6B and two FLF6G. All these vehicles had recently been repainted in United's poppy red and white livery, except for the FLF6Gs which remained in East Midland green and white, but

with United fleetnames; these two vehicles have since been withdrawn.

In February 1977 United added nine Leyland Nationals to its predominantly Bristol fleet, and these were allocated to the Town fleet. United was one of the last NBC subsidiaries to take delivery of the National, and consequently does not have any of the earlier Phase 1 type. Following an agreement between management and staff, one-man operation was introduced on the sea front service, and less extra staff were required during the summer months; in previous years a number of students had been employed as conductors.

One of the busiest routes during the summer is service 109, linking the Corner Cafe (North Sands) with the Spa (South Sands). The route, just over two miles long, follows the promenade most of the way, and is served by three Bristol VRTs at off-peak and four at peak times, plus duplicates depending on the demand; here the weather is a major factor. To strengthen the fleet of high-capacity one-man double-deckers, four Bristol VRT3s were diverted from Southdown and sent to Scarborough; they were numbered 709-712 and kept their original Southdown registrations, PUF 590-3R. These buses were consistently used on the 109 service and were well-liked by the one-man drivers, who referred to them as 'the flying PUFS'. As the sea front service only operates in the summer, it has no set timetable and

23

An ex-East Midland Leyland Leopard/Willowbrook 53-seater at the north end of Scarborough on the Whitby service.

runs at frequent intervals every day between 0900 and 2100. The smooth operation of the service is often hampered by the traffic congestion along the sea front as motorists manoeuvre into the parking spaces provided by the council along the main part of the route. On occasions the service has to be withdrawn as strong winds can whip large waves over the road, causing it to be dangerous. It seems a great pity that United has not introduced open-top double-deckers on this embracing and picturesque route, but the generally changeable weather and cool easterly sea breezes may have discouraged the company. Five of United's town services terminate at the Corner Cafe, and to control the numerous departures it is necessary to have an inspector on duty all day.

Several excursions and tours are operated during the summer, entailing morning, afternoon, evening and all-day tours on each day of the week except Saturdays. They include tours of Scarborough and Olives Mount, the North Yorkshire Moors steam railway, Flamingo Zoo, Hornsea Potteries, Castle Howard, the historic city of York, and the beautiful countryside of North Yorkshire. The departure point for the tours is the railway station forecourt, and bookings are taken at a small office next to the station entrance. The railway station is s tuated across the road from Valley Bridge bus station, and on the opposite side to them is the Westwood coach station, departure point for the bulk of the express services. East Yorkshire operates services to Scarborough from Humberside, the longest being the 2¾ hour journey from Hull via Bridlington. The service is jointly operated with United as far as Bridlington. East Yorkshire also provides a Thursday and Saturday service from Driffield to Scarborough. What is now the Westwood coach station used to be East Yorkshire's bus station, but in May 1970 that company moved in with United at Valley Bridge, releasing valuable space for express service departures and coach parking, with United assuming responsibility for running both Valley Bridge and Westwood. As a former BET company East Yorkshire offers a completely different selection of vehicles from United. It was still possible in 1977 to see the odd AEC Renown operating into Scarborough, and Daimler Fleetlines and Leyland Panthers were frequent visitors. More recent varieties are Bristol VRs, and Ford/Duple Dominant service buses working the Driffield service.

The third NBC operator to serve Scarborough is West Yorkshire, which used to operate from its own bus station/garage until 1969; in April of that year the company reorganised its operations and transferred everything to Valley Bridge. One service from

Scarborough to Flixton was transferred to United, and some of the vehicles and staff worked from Vernon Street. West Yorkshire is responsible for the operation of the composite services to York, Leeds, Bradford and Harrogate via Malton — which is now its closest operational depot to Scarborough.

Scarborough is a firm favourite with Scottish holidaymakers, many of them making the journey by coach. Eastern Scottish is one of the main operators which benefits from this traffic, and provides express services from both Glasgow and Edinburgh. The Friday night service is popular, arriving at Westwood coach station between 0600 and 0700 on Saturday mornings. At Valley Bridge United provides a refuelling service for the Scottish coaches as this facility is just not practical at Vernon Street garage at that time in the morning during the busy season.

Extended tour holiday coaches from Scotland, in particular Midland Bluebird and Northern, use Westwood as a base. Westwood is also the main coach park for vehicles associated with NBC, whether on express service or day excursion work. Independents and other operators are also allowed to park for a charge when there is room available. Hardwick's Services Ltd., part of the Wallace Arnold group of companies, operates a daily service from

Above: *A 1964 East Yorkshire AEC Renown with 74-seat Park Royal body on the Hull service.*

Below: *The only Mercedes-Benz in the Wallace Arnold fleet, an 0302 model, preparing to leave Scarborough on a full day tour.*

A Leyland Leopard/Plaxton Supreme of Skill's at William Street coach station operating the Market Harborough service.

Westwood to Ebberton, 14 miles away. The office and departure area are leased from United. Six Leyland Leopards with Plaxton Panorama coachwork are used; they are all one-man operated, and fitted out with 53 *bus* seats. They are garaged at Snainton, one of the villages en route to Ebberton. During the summer peak Saturdays the sheer volume of express services arriving and departing reveals the inadequacy of the coach station to absorb so many vehicles. This is further aggravated by the narrow access to the station from the main road. With the majority of departures leaving from temporary open stances, Westwood is not the most pleasant of places to be queueing for a coach, especially on a wet day.

Wallace Arnold tours have a strong foothold in Scarborough, providing excursions, tours, private hire and schools/works contracts. Fourteen coaches are based at the North Garage, Columbus Ravine, at the north side of the town. A mixed bag of coaches is operated, including Bedford YRQ, YMT and YRT models, one Leyland Leopard, one AEC Reliance and the sole Mercedes-Benz 0302 coach in the WA fleet. The company also has an engineering and servicing garage at Beaconsfield Street, on the other side of the town. A full range of excursions and tours are provided for visiting holidaymakers, and destinations are similar to those offered by United. Five of the Bedfords, painted in various liveries, are specially hired in for the summer season from dealers.

Wallace Arnold also supplies all the vehicles used to convey personnel to the RCA Fylingdale early warning station on the North Yorkshire Moors. The drivers, although trained by WA, are RCA employees. There are six Bedford 12-seat minibuses and ten old WA coaches, 1965 Leopards with Plaxton Panorama 49-seat centre-entrance coachwork. They are painted

in a dark grey livery with white and red relief, and have no fleetnames except for the small legal lettering along the bottom panel. These vehicles are based at various places where transport to this remote station is required. Some of the coaches are based at Scarborough, Whitby and Pickering.

Scarborough provides an adequate coach park for the numerous coaches that visit the resort during the peak season. Coaches from all parts of the Midlands, Yorkshire and the North-East bring in trippers by the thousand. William Street coach park is the main parking lot and can accommodate up to 220 coaches. An overflow coach park further away from the sea front, and is well signposted on all the main incoming roads. It is also the terminus for three independent express services. Barton operates a summer-only Market Harborough service X45, Norfolk Motor Services operates a summer-only Lowestoft /Caister/Norwich service, and Skills provides an all-year round service from Market Harborough via Leicester, Nottingham, York, Bridlington and Filey. All the express services depart from the parking area nearest the entrance/exit, with Skills commanding the top spot. Skills uses a variety of interesting coaches for its services, including Leyland Panthers, Volvos and Leyland Leopards, all with Plaxton coachwork.

In all, Scarborough is a truly interesting place to visit.

26

Plaxton Buses

Photographs by G. COXON

Plaxton combined a Highway body with a coach front to provide a service body for Bedford SB1 chassis, with raised floorline. This 1960 example, a 44-seat bus for Armstrong, Ebchester, was one of only six built.

Some independents had older front-engined chassis rebuilt and rebodied with Highway bus bodywork, like this AEC Regal III 39-seater built in 1958 for Ezra Laycock, Barnoldswick.

The Plaxton Highway bus body became very popular with independents, and the body suited most underfloor-engined chassis. This 45-seater for Howlett's (Quorn) Ltd was new in 1958 on Albion Aberdonian chassis.

27

Above: *From 1962 Plaxton produced the all-metal Derwent Mk I body. Most went to West Riding, seven on Leyland Leopard chassis, but there were three AEC Reliances, including this 1963 53-seater for Jones, Aberbeeg.*

Below: *This Daimler Roadliner SRC6 for AA, Ayr, was built at the same time as the first batch of Plaxton's new Derwent II body, which went to West Riding. A 52-seater, it was new in 1966.*

Journeys to Work. *An ex-Thames Valley Bristol LL6B of George Dew, Oldham, amid the mud and stone of his Buckton quarry near Oldham, April 1969.*

Warwickshire
School Buses

Photographs by T. W. MOORE

Below: *A former Rhondda AEC Regent V/MCW of G&G Coaches, Leamington, loads children from Leamington swimming baths.*

Opposite: *In 1975 this ex-Eastbourne Corporation AEC Regent V/East Lancs was operating on schools contracts for George's Coaches, Coventry.*

AEC double-deckers are popular with independent fleets operating school contract services in Warwickshire. These children, returning from an afternoon swimming lesson at Southam Junior School, in the cental area of Warwickshire, are unloading from a former East Kent AEC Regent V/Park Royal of Catteralls Coaches, Long Itchington, in November 1976.

Another reliable AEC double-decker at work on school services is the ex-East Yorkshire Bridgemaster owned by Priory Coaches, Leamington. It is pictured loading up a school swimming class in Leamington in September 1977.

32

Arriving at Stratford-on-Avon High School is Smith, Tysoe's AEC Renown 212 JUS. The bus was about to make its first pick-up at schools and colleges in the area in September 1977. It started life with another Smith — of Barrhead.

Loading up at Kineton High School, Smith, Tysoe has this ex-East Kent Park Royal-bodied AEC Regent V in its fleet providing transport to and from schools through the South Warwickshire villages.

In the north of Warwickshire, pupils at Atherstone High School have this very smart ex-Bristol Omnibus FLF Lodekka to transport them to and from school. The Lodekka was a new addition to the Deluxe Coaches fleet at Atherstone when pictured in September 1977.

Painted black and white, this former Glasgow Alexander-bodied Leyland Titan PD3/2 is seen at work for Terry's Coaches of Longford, providing transport fro the pupils at Kerseley Newlands High School, near Coventry.

Mid Warwickshire Motors of Balsall Common has three of these ex-London Transport AEC Merlins in its fleet. One of them makes its first drop in Burton Green on its way from Kenilworth Grammar School in October 1977, working a school service.

A vast amount of school work is operated by the bigger fleets, West Midlands PTE and Midland Red, in addition to the independent operators. This 1963 Midland Red Leyland Leopard with Willowbrook 53-seat bus body is working at Myton High School in Leamington, in July 1977.

West Side Story

JASPER PETTIE CA, MCIT, grew up with the large Western SMT fleet, and he recalls the vehicle variety which could be seen in the 1950s.

Western SMT is today, with over 900 vehicles, the largest constituent member of the Scottish Bus Group. To the enthusiast it presents a uniform and orderly image of operation — Alexander and Northern Counties bodied Daimler Fleetlines, together with Bristol Lodekkas, Albion Lowlanders and lowbridge Leyland PD3s dominate the double-deck fleet, while the bulk of the single deckers are Leyland Leopards with a growing number of Seddon Pennines and a smattering of Bristol REs — all with the ubiquitous Alexander Y-type body. More recently of course the Alexander T-type body has made its appearance and on the way out is the Bristol MW with Alexander 41-seat coach body, a combination unique to Western.

Yet this has by no means always been the case. Western, second only in size to Alexanders until the latter's empire was fragmented in 1961, has had a collection of vehicles which for sheer variety can easily rival that of its larger associate. Formed in 1932 around the nucleus of Midland Bus Services Ltd, of

Airdrie, the company expanded steadily during the 1930s and 1940s by the takeover of numerous operators, at first mainly in Ayrshire and Renfrewshire but later all over the West of Scotland. Surprisingly, however, until recently very little had been written about either its operations or its vehicles. Prior to 1949, only half-hearted attempts at any form of fleet numbering were tried and it is possibly because of this that research into early information was extremely complicated.

It was in 1953 when our family moved to Ayrshire that as a schoolboy I first became acquainted with the red Western buses. Although I did not realise it at the time, the company was settling down to a period of comparative calm after a veritable plethora of takeovers and mergers as well as heavy purchases of both new and second hand vehicles in the immediate postwar period. Nationalisation had come in 1949 and also in that year the three operating subsidiaries were wound up, these being W. & R. Dunlop of Greenock, Greenock Motor Services and Rothesay Tramways, the last being a statutory company by then operating only buses. This move added over 160 buses to the 600-strong fleet. The Caledonian Omnibus Co Ltd, of Dumfries, already nationalised with the rest of the Tilling organisation in 1948, came into the Western

Left: *A 1946 Guy Arab II with 6LW engine and Northern Counties 56-seat body is seen working for Western SMT on an Ayr local service. In earlier years it had been a stalwart on the Glasgow-Ayr via Kilmarnock service.*

Right: *One of the famous Albion Venturers used on the services from Glasgow to Ayr and Stranraer. The 53-seat bodies were by Alexander.*

Ayr bus station in the late 1950s, with AY1010, Western's first Guy Arab IV and first tin front bus, dating from 1952. Northern Counties 53-seat bodywork was fitted.

fold on 31 December 1949 and this brought the fleet total to over 900. The following year the company purchased the fleet of Young's Bus Service Ltd of Paisley and its associate Paisley & District, the combined vehicle strength of which had reached 141.

The vehicles taken over from these operators varied enormously in size, make and form, and many had reached the end of their useful working lives. Shortly after, the opportunity was taken by the Scottish group to purchase a large quantity of wartime Guy Arabs from London Transport and Western received a sizeable allocation of these which took to the road in various rebuilt and unrebuilt forms to replace some of the old worn-out machines it had inherited.

Our village was well served by stage routes in those days, the most frequent of these being the Glasgow-Ayr via Kilmarnock service and I discovered that the vehicles of three depots — Ayr, Newton Mearns and Kilmarnock — were regular performers. Ayr principally employed the 18 Alexander-bodied Albion Venturers, two of which were new in 1947 with Burlingham bodies from Ribble Titans and had been rebodied by Alexander in 1949 at the time the other 16 were being built. These handsome machines had had their Albion engines replaced by Gardner 6LW units at an early stage and had a very short life, being

withdrawn by 1961. I remember how well-appointed the interiors of these vehicles were, making use of much heavily-varnished woodwork, and a feature which sticks in my mind was the ornate wooden 'W' symbol mounted on the lower deck front bulkhead. Ayr also had a large allocation of Guy Arabs, and many of these were to be seen on the route at times, although it was mainly the 6LW-engined highbridge Northern Counties-bodied ASD and BAG-registered batches. The 5LW-engined buses (which included the ex-LTE examples) were mainly confined to Ayr locals. Ayr also had a number of Leyland TS7s, which had started life as coaches, some for the London service and which had been fitted during the War with utility Alexander lowbridge bodies, becoming TD4s in the process. While these were also mainly employed on local services, on odd occasions one could be seen working the Glasgow service, although as the 1950s progressed this became a rarer and rarer occurrence. One vehicle conspicuous by its appearance was AY1010 (ESD 208), the first Guy Arab Mk IV and the first tin-front bus in the fleet. It had a handsome lowbridge Northern Counties body, and was followed in the ensuing years by further batches of Arab IVs, some with Alexander bodies and these replaced the Albions and older Guys on the Glasgow-Ayr route.

A word or two about the fleet numbering system might be appropriate here. In 1949 Western allocated a number to each vehicle starting at 1 and progressing broadly in an age sequence, the oldest with the lowest numbers. Vehicles taken over from subsidiaries took the next available numbers and it was rare for a number to be used more than once. Ex-Young's buses had 2000 added to their existing numbers. Each number was preceded by two letters, the first denoting the depot and the other the type of vehicle, generally the first letter of the make name for a single-deck and the last for a double-deck. Thus AY stood for Ayr (depot) GuY (double-deck).

Newton Mearns had at that time an all-Leyland double-deck fleet and the vehicles most frequently used on the Ayr service were a batch of Leyland PD1s new in 1949 with Strachans bodies but which in 1952 had been replaced by ECW lowbridge bodies. Some of these had VS registrations and had originated with the Greenock Motor Services subsidiary. Supplementing these were lowbridge Northern Counties-bodied Leyland PD1s new in 1948. This situation lasted until 1955 when new PD2s were placed on the service and from then on successive batches of PD2s and then PD3s were used.

Kilmarnock depot's contribution to the Glasgow-Ayr route was confined to only two or three duties per day, and these were invariably Daimlers, usually from two batches: the 1948 CVA6s with lowbridge Northern Counties bodywork, all of which were allocated to Kilmarnock, or the 1950 batch of CVG6s ordered by Young's but delivered to Western — KR 912-7 (XS 7018-23) also with Northern Counties bodies but to highbridge pattern. Other vehicles occasionally appeared — sometimes a utility Daimler

or a prewar Leyland TD but these were rare. By the mid-1950s these were also largely replaced by the all-conquering PD2.

Ayr depot's allocation also included duties on the Glasgow-Stranraer service which at that time was Britain's longest stage carriage route served by double-deckers. Albions and Guys of the batches previously mentioned were used, but for a short time in 1955 Guy Arab LUF saloons were placed on the service but soon withdrawn, as passenger loadings tended to exceed available capacity. These were Alexander-bodied 44-seaters.

The other route serving our village was also a long stage service, being that from Glasgow to Dumfries via Kilmarnock and Cumnock, later linked with journeys from Dumfries to Carlisle to provide a through facility. In the early 1950s Cumnock depot operated AEC Regent IIIs with Northern Counties lowbridge bodies which were always immaculately turned out. By 1955 these began to be replaced by AEC Regal IVs displaced from the London express service and reseated as buses, the toilets being removed in the process. These vehicles had originally been destined for Scottish Omnibuses and had indeed been registered in Edinburgh as HWS 927-940; after rebuilding they were split between Cumnock and Inchinnan depots.

Although my interest in buses had developed before our move to Ayrshire it was nurtured and expanded by the veritable pageant of assorted types of vehicles then in service. In retrospect I am glad to have had the opportunity to sample at first hand makes and types of buses which within a few years would only be a memory. I remember one Saturday travelling on an ex-Caledonian prewar Dennis Lancet DS841

(CSM 770) which had somehow found its way from Dumfries and was working through to Glasgow. The odd Bristol L and even once a TD1 (!) from the same stable worked the service all the way through; presumably this was when Cumnock was experiencing a shortage of vehicles of one kind or another. In addition a couple of vehicle-journeys per day were linked with the Glasgow-Ayr via Troon service and occasionally a Johnstone-based bus put in an appearance. I particularly remember a journey on an English Electric-bodied Albion decker ex-Young's JN 2108 (XS 4769); it gave a disappointingly ponderous performance and was definitely on its last legs.

As far as the regular vehicles were concerned if there was a common link in the variety it was to be found in the bodywork manufacture. Northern Counties had been a favoured supplier to Western for many years and their distinctive postwar styles were to be found in both highbridge and lowbridge forms on a wide variety of AEC, Daimler, Guy and Leyland models. Youngs had also standardised on this body supplier.

Gradually, as I began to appreciate the size of Western's operating territory, it became apparent that in this period of settling down Western was endeavouring to rationalise vehicle allocations at its depots. Kilmarnock and Johnstone, for instance, shared all the Daimlers in the fleet, the former having all the utilities (including the few ex-Young's and Greenock examples) as well as the CVA6s. By and large most of the other ex-Young's vehicles remained at Johnstone and these included most of the CVG6s, together with many of the 1952 batch of Alexander and Northern Counties-bodied machines purchased

new. Some of the ex-Young's Guys were later allocated to Dumfries and one or two to Ayr, both depots having sizeable allocations of Guys of all types including many ex-London Transport. The other depot operating Guys was Greenock which had all but one of the ex-Greenock Motor Services Arabs. The 'odd-Guy-out' was AY 726 (VS 4357) at Ayr, which had been fitted with a utility Park Royal body from an ex-LTE Guy. While on the subject of rebodying, it can be recalled that Western embarked on a programme of fitting new lowbridge Alexander bodies and both low and highbridge ECW bodies to utility Guys. While the vehicles selected for treatment appeared to be numerically at random, the condition of the original body was basically the determining factor.

Newton Mearns had a wonderful collection of prewar Leyland TDs which were used for the network of short-distance services from Glasgow to the south, namely, Barrhead, Nitshill, Clarkston, Mearnskirk and Spiersbridge. These ranged from Leyland highbridge TD5s, some of which were rebuilt by ECW in the early 1950s to TD4s which had the ubiquitous postwar Northern Counties lowbridge body. A number of other TD4s had utility Alexander bodies, and were rebuilt from TS7 single-deckers during the War, these being found in penny numbers in most Western depots. In addition to all these and the PD1s mentioned there were allocated about 30 of the 45 all-Leyland PD1s delivered in 1947/48. Amid all these several 'characters' stick out in my memory. The first of these was a solitary TD7, a refugee from the Young's fleet, MD 2129 (XS 5480) of 1942. Its original Pickering utility body had been considerably rebuilt, with rubber-mounted windows flush with the body sides, rather like a forerunner of the dreaded

MCW Orion style. Altogether it was a very sorry-looking vehicle. It rarely ventured out, and when it did it had a most peculiar engine note, not at all like an 8.6 litre. Another vehicle with an odd engine was MD 2169 (XS 6463) the only other ex-Young vehicle, which was a PD2 with highbridge Northern Counties body of 1948. I later learned that it had been fitted with a 7.4 litre E181 engine, hence its transfer from Johnstone which had no vehicles with this engine configuration. For many years it was a stalwart on the Glasgow-Mearnskirk via Giffnock service.

A surprise came during 1957 when three Leyland TD3s and one TD4 were transferred from Greenock New to Greenock Motor Services. The postwar Alexander bodies on the 1934 TD3s, MD 666-8 (VS 2603-5) were similar in outline to the original Leyland body on the TD4, MD 678 (VS 3074), new in 1936. They eked out their last days on rush-hour duties, and could always be distinguished by the word *LOCAL* in the glass above the destination screen, rather than *WESTERN*. The use of this distinction was confined mainly to ex-Young's and GMS vehicles at their original depots.

In addition to Guys, Ayr depot had a fair-sized allocation of Leyland TD deckers, mainly TD4 ex-TS7 'utilities', but one interesting machine was AD50 (CS 2024) which had been rebuilt as late as 1950 and fitted with an elegant Burlingham highbridge body, the only one of this make owned by Western. It was of that manufacturer's 'rococo' style with heavily radiused window corners. In addition to the Albions mentioned there were four ex-Young's exiles, Venturers new in 1938 whose English Electric bodies had been exchanged for ECW lowbridge ones in 1952/53. Ayr also had a fair-sized fleet of single-deckers, comprising some all-Guy Arab Mk III saloons and Leyland Lion LT5As and LT7s with postwar Brush coachwork and 7.4 litre engines used to reintroduce the London express service after the War but now downgraded to stage work. There was also a batch of Burlingham coach-bodied PS1s for tour and private hire work, some in the black/white livery.

AEC vehicles were entirely confined to Cumnock, Dumfries, Greenock and Inchinnan, although the Regal IV London coaches were originally stabled at Kilmarnock. Interesting among these were a batch of Regal Is, some of which had been converted to double-deck and fitted with Bristol lowbridge bodies, similar in outline to the ECW product. There were also some coaches, Burlingham-bodied Regal IIIs and Regal Is with Brush bodies similar to the LT5As, mostly at Cumnock, Greenock and Inchinnan.

Kilmarnock, as already mentioned, had Western's entire stock of utility Daimlers, and these comprised CWG5s as well as the more usual CWA6s. Of these

vehicles I particularly remember KR 244-7 (ASD 120-3), CWG5s of 1943 with Massey bodies which had been substantially rebuilt by Western using Leyland-style framing and windows. The result was most un-Massey and enhanced the appearance considerably. One Massey-bodied Guy at Ayr, AY 203 (ASD 95) was similarly treated. KR 257 (ASD 967), a CWA6, had had its Brush body replaced by a Park Royal one of similar vintage from an ex-LTE Arab. Three other CWA6s which came in for more drastic treatment were KR 210/1/41 (ASD 351, 414, VS 4309). They were rebodied by ECW, resulting in a unique combination. Western also had an interesting method of identifying engine types in Daimlers at a glance. The Gardner engined (i.e. CWG5, CVG6) examples had chrome radiators, and those with AEC 7.7 litre (most of the CWA6 and all the CVA6) had black-painted radiators with the top tank fluting polished brass. Quite a number of the Leyland TDs throughout the company also had beautiful polished brass radiators and Kilmarnock's allocation was no exception. One such vehicle was KD 75 (CS 4498) which had an interesting Leyland lowbridge body. Constructed in 1942, it had been supplied 'loose' to Alexander as a shell. Alexander had then fitted it out and placed it on the TD4 chassis to replace the original highbridge Leyland body which had been damaged by fire.

For several years the oldest double-deckers in the Western fleet were stationed at Kilmarnock. These were Leyland TD3s of 1934, KD 13-15 (CS 124-6), which had utility Alexander bodies fitted in 1945. Two other TD3s with similar bodies were KD 16/7 but had originated with Sheffield as WJ 9090/5 and had come to Western via Alexander which had not operated

Left: *This Daimler CVG6 with Northern Counties body was one of six ordered by Young but delivered shortly after the take-over, and which spent their entire working lives at Kilmarnock. KR912 is seen in Fenwick in 1958; it was withdrawn in 1964.*

Right: *One of the fleet of AEC-engined Maudslay Marathon III coaches taken over from Young; this was one of two with half-cab Scottish Aviation coachwork, seen in black and white livery at Largs.*

them. Their torque convertors had been removed and standard crash gearboxes fitted. One other Leyland was the subject of an interesting rebody while at Kilmarnock. KD 105 (CS 5257), a TD4, had its utility Alexander body removed in 1958 and replaced by that from GD 733 (BU 8257) an ex-Oldham TD3; this was a Leyland-style Alexander body new in 1948. It ran for less than a year in this form and indeed the reason behind rebodying such an elderly bus in this way has never come to light.

Kilmarnock's single-deck fleet was larger than that of most other depots, and the bulk of these were 1948 Burlingham-bodied Leyland PS1 saloons. These were operated on several local services notably Bonnyton-Culzean Crescent, because of a low railway bridge; similar obstacles on the Glasgow via Barrhead route also required single-deck vehicles. These were supplemented by several of the 16-strong 1949 PS1 deliveries, these having Alexander bodies.

I feel that it is perhaps appropriate to give a brief resumé of the Western coach fleet as it was then to complete this survey of my observations. Western's policy then was to retain what amounted to two separate fleets of coaches in the distinctive and famous black/white livery. One of course was that which served the Glasgow-London express service. As already mentioned this was restarted after the War using rebodied Leyland Lion LTs with 7.4 litre engines from various sources. By 1952, these had been downgraded and replaced by the AEC Regal IVs and a batch of Guy Arab UFs, all with toilets. The Guys were nicknamed 'bombers' because of their high unladen weight of over 8 tons and served on the London service well into the mid 1960s. London coaches were stabled mainly at Kilmarnock, Newton

Mearns and Johnstone depots.

The other black/white 'fleet' was really a pool of coaches retained for day and extended tours and important private hire work. As this side of the business started to pick up in the postwar period, the first coaches so allocated were Burlingham-bodied PS1s in 1948, supplemented by similar bodies on reconditioned TD4 double-deck chassis ex-Glasgow and Sheffield. More followed in 1949, again on PS1 chassis and also on AEC Regal IIIs. The Maudslay coaches acquired with the Young's takeover were also repainted black/white and were often to be seen working private hires from Johnstone. The majority had Brockhouse full-front coachwork, but two carried rather attractive half cab bodies by Scottish Aviation. Gradually as the 1950s progressed the Guy UFs and LUFs and then Bristol LSs and MWs arrived, these vehicles were downgraded to the cream/red roof and flash of the 'dual purpose' fleet which were used for private hire work as well as more mundane stage operations.

Western's 1950s policy of quickly replacing non-standard vehicles began to bite into the ranks, and soon many of the old faithfuls had gone, to be replaced by Leyland PD2s and PD3s and Bristol Lodekkas, none of which seemed to have the same individual characteristics and quirks, and now many of these have in their turn been replaced by Fleetlines and Leopards. It is all the more unfortunate that none of them has survived to be preserved — indeed there are few Northern-Counties-bodied vehicles in preservation at all. It is hoped however that this short account has served to bring to light something of the colour and the atmosphere that was unique to Western in this most interesting period.

Second-hand Trolleybuses

Photographs by R. L. WILSON

Left: This Sunbeam F4 trolleybus started life in 1948 as a single-decker on the Mexborough & Swinton system. It was bought by Bradford Corporation in 1962, and this East Lancs 66-seat forward entrance body was fitted the same year.

Above: South Shields Corporation bought this 1950 Sunbeam F4 with East Lancs body from St Helens Corporation in 1959. It is seen in the Market Place in 1963.

Right: An ex-St Helens BUT 9611T with East Lancs 63-seat body, one of eight which passed to Bradford Corporation in 1959. It is now preserved.

Left: Another second-hand Bradford acquisition, an ex-Llanelly & District 1946 Karrier W, bought in 1956. It was rebodied by East Lancs the same year.

Right: New in 1950, this BUT 9611T with Northern Coachbuilders 54-seat body passed from Grimsby-Cleethorpes to Walsall in 1960. The body was lengthened and rebuilt by Walsall to become a 69-seater.

This Maidstone Corporation Sunbeam W with MCW 56-seat body was new to Hastings Tramways in 1948. Hastings Tramways was a subsidiary of Maidstone & District, and was absorbed into M&D in 1957. This trolleybus passed to the Corporation in 1959 when the system closed in 1959.

Another second-hand purchase for Maidstone Corporation in 1959 was this former Brighton Corporation BUT 9611T with 56-seat Weymann body, seen here in 1960. It is now preserved.

On the last full day of operation on the Teesside Municipal Transport trolleybus system, in April 1971, an ex-Reading Corporation 1961 Sunbeam F4A with 68-seat Burlingham forward-entrance body, now preserved.

Another ex-Reading Sunbeam, now preserved, is this 1950 Sunbeam S7 with Park Royal 68-seat body. It is seen running under the wires at the Sandtoft Trolleybus Museum.

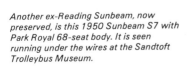

Walsall Corporation bought several of these Sunbeam F4s with Park Royal 56-seat bodies from Ipswich Corporation in 1962.

Preserved as a reminder of the Portsmouth Corporation trolleybus network, this 1934 AEC 661T with English Electric 50-seat body was photographed at the Montagu Motor Museum at Beaulieu in 1966.

46

West Side Story. *A 1950 Daimler CVG6/Northern Counties of Western SMT working a local service in Kilmarnock. It was one of six ordered by Young's, Paisley, but delivered after the take-over to Western.*

Paisley Patterns. *A Leyland Atlantean AN68/1R with West Yorkshire PTE-style Roe 76-seat body delivered in 1977 to Cunningham's, Paisley.*

Beside the Seaside, beside the Sea. *Unmistakeably Blackpool, with one of the English Electric-built 'balloon' 94-seat trams — as much a part of the Blackpool scene as the Tower in the background.*

MARTIN J. PERRY

TEME WORK

With the proprietor at the wheel, one of Morris's assorted AECs heads on to the Teme Bridge at Knightwick on a school contract. Duple (Northern) Continental coachwork is carried, and the photo was taken in 1975.

It all begins high on Cilfaesty Hill, one of the mighty green peaks of the Marches, where the Salopian Clun Forest rolls out of England to become the Montgomeryshire Wales of the Kerry Hills. Up here, where sheep outnumber humans and roads become blocked by summer's tourists and winter's snows, the tiny mountain streams run and merge until they form the infant River Teme, beginning its rural meanderings eastward into England and eventually to the great Severn river itself. Now the new County of Powys, but for ever Radnorshire, the Teme begins its journey that will pass a number of places of interest to the errant enthusiast.

Only a matter of six miles from the windswept heights of Cilfaesty is the tiny hamlet of Velindre, notable for being home to a former London Transport Guy GS. Here, in the tidy garage of J. Lakelin, MXX 361 has escaped the hustle of the Home

Counties, and now spends leisurely hours carrying the children of the village school. In a smart, almost streamlined dark green and cream garb, MXX rubs daily shoulders with grey Ferguson tractors, a Thames/Yeoman coach and a pair of Bedford/Plaxtons. In her twelfth year at Velindre, MXX shows no intention of retiring just yet, but no doubt the day will dawn when she is put out to grass with the remains, behind the garage, of one of the erstwhile ubiquitous Ministry of Supply Bedford OB/Duple buses.

Descending a further nine miles down the twisting valley, we come to Knighton — 'second city' of Radnorshire and a thriving centre for markets and light industry. At one time, de-population threatened this ancient town, built on Offa's Dyke, but today the old values mix freely with new populations working in clothing or agricultural machinery factories, and this industry and the

larger schools support the ten-vehicle fleet of Owen's Motors Ltd. To be found just over the Teme bridge in Skyborry Road, Owen's clean grey and blue Bedfords work out over the surrounding hills on contracts each day, whilst stage carriages run to Presteigne and The Pound on market days. Until 1962, Knighton had two established operators: Owen's (who had started in 1929 with a Chevrolet LM), and the smart Bedford and Austin fleet of Williams & Wooding (who ran the Presteigne service and held excursion and tour licences). December 1962, however, saw the consolidation of Owen's business, with the purchase of the Williams and Wooding enterprise. Although in the late 1940s Owen's had acquired a number of new Bedford OBs, it was not until 1972 that a new Bedford SB5/Duple Vega became the first new coach in 22 years. Three Bedford CF minibuses and

49

CUJ 308C, an ex-Whittle SB/Bella Vega. Usual operation of the Ludlow service is in the hands of a Ford R192 service bus with severe Strachan bodywork; this was joined in 1974 by a grant Bedford/ Dominant coach. For the contracts come a fine selection — a Bedford C-type 'Humpty-Dumpty' coach, an ex-Army SB/Strachan bus, and a hefty AEC/Duple Britannia coach. Finally there are three 12-seaters (of Bedford, Ford and BMC manufacture !) for the real back roads.

The village bus stop, on the Teme bridge opposite Griffiths' garage, also sees vehicles of Leominster-based Primrose Motors, working stage carriage to their home town, and school contracts by Lugg Valley Motors, also from Leominster. (Attentive readers, will, by now, have noted the local popularity of their rivers and their valleys in fleet names !)

Out of Leintwardine, the road climbs high above the meandering Teme, and whilst the river wanders through Downton-on-the-Rock and Bromfield, the highway takes us over the wooded slopes of Bringewood Chase, and down across the Shropshire border into Ludlow. Dominated by its ancient ruined castle, and focal point for all of South Shropshire, Ludlow is the base for the smart, very modern fleet of Corvedale Motors. And yet again, we cannot escape river valleys, for 'Corvedale' is but another way of saying 'the valley of the River Corve' — itself a tributary of the Teme.

The interesting history of

assorted SBs and YRQs now comprise the workforce, with the CFs forming an important part of the daily scene — this is an area where some school contracts, although up to 20 miles in duration, carry only a handful of children from the scattered hill farms, and the small bus is a necessity. Knighton's cattle market car-park also serves as the town bus station, and here may be seen the Ford/Plaxton coach of Knighton's other operator, G. Watkins. Working into town on the main route from Ludlow will be a member of the Teme Valley Motors fleet (of which more later), whilst on a Thursday a green Bedford (or possibly a big Seddon) of Price's 'Clun Valley' will work down on stage carriage over the hills from Newcastle and Clun ('the loveliest places under the sun . . .') !

Overnight, one or two of the motley collection of works buses owned by J. P. Wood's 'Chukie

Chickens' will rest here — perhaps former London RF555 or former Oxford, North Western or Maidstone Reliances. Latest arrivals to the garish turquoise and white livery are former Southern Vectis Bristol saloons.

Out of Knighton, it is the main A4113 road that follows the valley of the Teme into England and the Herefordshire village of Leintwardine. Until recently supporting two operators, now only the appropriately named 'Teme Valley Motors' fleet of W. & C. A. Griffiths remains. Teme Valley commenced in 1952, operating school contracts and later excursions and tours. Eight years later two stage routes were acquired from Corvedale Motors of Ludlow , and today the main road Knighton to Ludlow route is still very active, in the hands of the patriotic red, white and blue coaches — a livery that was inherited with the purchase of

One of two Guy GSs operated by J. P. Wood, MXX leaves Craven Arms in 1970, bound for Ludlow.

Below: *Waiting in the wet in Ludlow's Castle Square, the upright Strachan-bodied Ford R192 service bus employed regularly by Teme Valley on its main Ludlow-Knighton service in March 1971.*

Corvedale Motors begins in 1930, over forty miles from Ludlow. In the south-Herefordshire village of Pontrilas, Mr W. E. Morgan had established bus operations in 1926, and by 1929 had commenced a Hereford-Leominster service. At the same time, he moved his base to Hereford, and sold the original Pontrilas concern to Mr E. E. Williams. Mr Morgan (trading as 'Wye Valley Motors'!!) in Hereford, expanded northwards and by 1931 had built up trunk routes to Shrewsbury, Bridgnorth and Ludlow, whilst down in Pontrilas Mr Williams was running buses to Hereford and Abergavenny. Over the following four years, and through the maze of applications and claims that followed the 1930 Road Traffic Act, the Wye Valley business established services well into Shropshire, and opened a depot in Ludlow for these operations. Back in Pontrilas, ill-health had forced Mr Williams to reduce his commitments, and in 1936, Morgan's Wye Valley acquired the majority of the Williams vehicles and services. However, three years later, Mr Williams moved north to Ludlow, and there took over the Wye Valley Shropshire operations, and adopted 'Corvedale' as the fleetname for his new enterprise. Wartime demands, and the acquisition of various small local operators, saw great expansions at Ludlow, and whilst a number of routes were sold (notably to the

erstwhile Radnorshire Motor Services and Midland Red), the 1950s established Corvedale as an undertaking of importance. The full story of the origins and growth of this business make a fascinating subject in themselves, but there cannot be room here for greater detail.

Another facet of the Corvedale business under Mr Williams ownership was the very large number of vehicles, both new and second-hand, that passed through the company, for buses were both operated and traded. A huge total of 286 vehicles was operated between 1939 and 1966, some staying for only a matter of weeks. In 1966, Mr Williams retired, and control of

Corvedale passed jointly to Yeomans of Hereford and Whittles of Highley, both well-known concerns, and for a while 'Yeomans-Corvedale' fleetnames were carried. Three years later, full control passed to the Whittle group, and today the fleet (based in Fishmore Road) consists of smart Bedford VAS, YLQ and YMT coaches with Duple Dominant coachwork, all in a tidy green and silver livery. Stage operations still figure well, with a Ludlow Town Service and routes to Tenbury, Cleobury, Abdon and the Clee Hill, along with schools, works and excursions. One of the works services carries staff to and from the BBC Transmitting station at Woofferton, four miles away,

operating daily throughout the year. Another noteworthy service is a stage operation to Wolverhampton, on the first Wednesday of the month, and to all home matches of the Wanderers football club — this latter as a public service, and not just restricted to soccer devotees! Until recently, services headed south to the Herefordshire villages of Wigmore and Orleton, but these have transferred to Primrose of Leominster, whose bright yellow and white machines now regularly reach Ludlow.

Ludlow's bus parking area, beneath the grey walls of the castle, is host to the Corvedale, Teme Valley and Primrose routes, along with stage operations by E. Austin of Aston Diddlebury (whose SB coaches make journeys in on alternate Mondays), and Arthur Boulton's Saturday service from the Church Stretton area (again with SB/Duple coaches as the mainstay, but on rare occasions his Van Hool bodied Bedford VAL, or Van Hool-McArdle Ford coaches — unusual choices for such a rural concern).

Midland Red established a garage in Ludlow in January 1951, and this still serves local routes with single and double-deck allocation, amounting to about a dozen vehicles — the scope of this article, however, must preclude greater detail.

Passing under the ancient Ludford bridge, the Teme now heads south-east and forms the boundary between Salop and Worcestershire, and just into this latter county is the market town of Tenbury Wells. Hopes to exploit the medicinal waters of this Edwardian 'spa' failed, and today it remains a market centre with a strong agricultural leaning. Although a town of over 2,000 inhabitants, no large psv undertakings are centred here (indeed, a solitary BMC JU minibus is Tenbury's one inmate), but daily stage and contract operations bring vehicles from Corvedale, Midland Red, M&M (another Whittle subsidiary with yellow and silver coaches) and Yarranton Bros.

To learn more of the last-named business, we must follow the Teme Valley downstream a further six miles, to find the Tenbury area's main coach business in the village of Eardiston.

Here, the tidy white and green Yarranton Bros. coaches are based, using Eardiston Coaches as a fleetname, and carrying the legend 'Yarrantons of Tenbury Wells' — the Town in the Orchard' on their boot doors, reflecting the fruit-growing agriculture of this part of the Teme's course. Established in 1919 with a Thornycroft BT 20-seat bus, the three Yarranton brothers built up several village market day routes, mostly centred on Tenbury, along with a daily Tenbury-Worcester service that still merits three journeys per weekday. Although Thornycrofts were popular during the 1920s and 30s, Bedford became the norm during the postwar years, and today the fleet is wholly Bedford or Ford ranging from a Transit minibus to 53-seat VAL and Ford coaches. Bell Punch tickets continue in use, printed in decimal values — something of a rarity in these days of one-man operation and the farebox.

The last miles of the Teme see the river in old age, following a sluggish course through hopyards, pasture meadows and the orchards of its lower valley. Under Stanford Bridge, where one of Morris's blue and cream fleet from Bromyard may be waiting to collect timber workers, and down through Shelsley Walsh, famous for its motor hill-climb. Under Ham Bridge, and past the village of Martley, whose large school attracts vehicles from Bromyard (whence Morris's send their assorted AECs) or coaches from Martley's own operators, G. Rogers, whose green and cream Fords and Bedfords await the four o'clock bell. Beneath the towering sleepness of

A Whittle group purchase, ostensibly for the narrow lanes around Ludlow, a 29-seat Duple-bodied Bedford VAS, built to the narrow 7ft 6in width.

Ankerdine Hill, whose 1 in 6 gradients sadly no longer echo the exhaust of the former East Midland Leyland PD2 of Morris's. However, the parishes of Knightwick and Lulsley mark the continuing passage of our river, and here Morris's weekday route from Bromyard to Worcester serves the scattered homes, offering a Plaxton Supreme-bodied AEC Reliance and Leyland Leopard. School contracts call for older stock, and thus a former West Riding Reliance or an ex-Maidstone Reliance saloon pound their daily beats. The lanes here are also served by Bromyard-based Silver Star — a name suggesting Atlantean coaches, but in reality bringing a variety of Transit minicoaches in a smart red/cream/black livery on schools and works commitments, once again emphasising the vitality of the small psv in such an area. Now, within an ace of its confluence with the murky waters of the Severn, the Teme passes the wide flood meadows of Leigh and Bransford until it empties into Sabrina's wider flow and our journey is at an end. From its source high in the Welsh Marches, to its demise near the Midland bustle of Worcester, the Teme Valley has offered some of Britain's finest landscape, and much to satisfy the intinerant enthusiast.

Curiouser and Curiouser/2

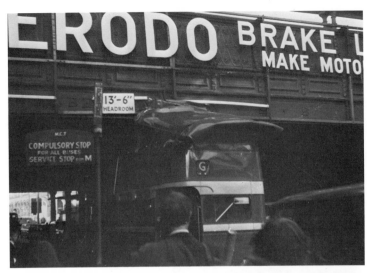

Compulsory Stop! Ferodo brake linings or not, this was the last day in passenger service for this Middlesbrough Corporation Guy Arab, in 1966.

The upper half of a Salford Corporation MCW-bodied Daimler CVG6 is carried into the Drill Hall on Great Clowes Street in 1951 on the occasion of the undertaking's Golden Jubilee exhibition. The lower half was already in position, ready for re-mating.

A horse with a sunshade and a six-wheel Italian trolleybus in Genoa.

Beside the Seaside, Beside the Sea

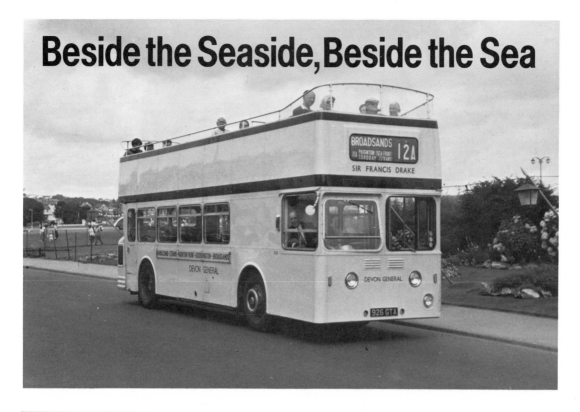

A nostalgic look at the delights of the seaside and its buses, by GAVIN BOOTH, self-confessed enthusiast for the British seaside, vulgarity and all.

You would be forgiven for thinking that after living for 15 years right by the sea — literally within sight, sound, smell and even spray of the sea — I would head resolutely inland on my summer holiday. Not a bit of it. In fact, for the last few years I have rarely had a holiday that hasn't been spent at least within easy reach of the sea.

The seaside to me means the often-faded pleasures of the traditional British seaside resort — sea, sand, funfairs, piers, lively crowds, noise and good honest vulgarity. Oh yes — and buses. Seaside buses, with or without roofs, have always seemed to be an integral part of the holiday, an important part of the atmosphere. My favourites among the seaside buses were always the municipal fleets, where the peak periods were reckoned in weeks of the year rather than hours of the day; where staff and vehicles were fully stretched over those few holiday weeks, coping patiently with the constant two-way traffic of over-laden holidaymakers. On fine mornings, the exodus

would be uniformly beach-bound; by early evening the reverse rush was on, with hungry hordes bound for *Mon Repos* (hot and cold in all rooms) for meat and two veg.

I was amazed to discover how many of Britain's best-known holiday resorts I had contrived to visit over the years. To be more specific I discovered with a certain amount of patriotic shame how many of *England's* best-known holiday resorts figured predominantly in the list; our Scottish resorts tend to lack the razzamatazz of their English counterparts — as a Scot I should, perhaps, be grateful, but as a seaside enthusiast it makes for longer journeys. North Wales, I fear, is still largely unknown territory, in spite of the twin attractions of big, busy resorts and narrow-gauge railways. Someday, perhaps.

England's south coast has always been my favourite; the resorts there seem to know how to make the most of themselves. I spent a most enjoyable holiday at Bournemouth in 1961, when the trolleybus system was still intact — in fact Bournemouth's, and Britain's, last new trolleybuses did not enter service until late in 1962.

The Bournemouth trolleybus system had replaced trams between 1933 and 1936, and many of the 1934-36 fleet of Park Royal-bodied Sunbeam MS2s remained in active service. These were being replaced by the final batches of handsome Weymann-bodied Sunbeam MF2Bs, some of which were still fairly new. There were also ex-Brighton Corporation BUTs with Weymann bodies, which looked very much at home in the Bournemouth fleet.

The motor bus fleet was equally interesting, with unrebuilt pre-war and wartime vehicles running alongside similar open-toppers, and newer buses which were still being built to the unusual Bournemouth two-door layout.

I had the chance to sample some of the older vehicles in open-top form — indulging my weakness for things topless. At Alum Chine I boarded 1943 Guy Arab/Weymann open-topper 38 running on route 12, the Coastal Service to Hengistbury Head. As I sank on to the wooden seat, the vehicle reluctantly started the long climb from the Chine terminus. Just as I thought — and secretly hoped — that the incline might prove too much for the 5LW engine, and the bus might stall, 38 took a cowardly right-hand turn on to a flat stretch. I was not to be disappointed, though.

After collecting the bulk of its 56 passengers at Bournemouth Pier, 38 toiled up towards Boscombe, and then left the direct route to make its scheduled descent into Boscombe Chine. The effect of slaving over a hot Gardner must have been too much for the driver, since three attempts to climb out of the Chine failed, stalling 38 a fraction of the way up the hill each time. Edging it back by brake after its third failure, the embarrassed driver resigned his cab to an ever-ready inspector who took over the controls and slowly brought it to the summit. My journey back to Bournemouth was on a delightful open-top Leyland Titan TD5 of 1939 vintage, admittedly a lightly-loaded one, which had no problems with the hills.

Rival seaside buses at Bournemouth in 1961 were Hants & Dorset's heavily-rebuilt utility Bristol K5Gs which bounced between the bus station and Lymington and Sandbanks, so naturally I had to sample them.

Further along the coast in 1961, I encountered more open-toppers at Portsmouth. The buses, Leyland Titan TD4s with English Electric bodies, were interesting, but the route was not, and lacked the scenery needed. As if to compensate, Portsmouth Corporation was still running enclosed Leyland TD4s with vee-fronted Leyland bodywork — a rare combination by that time — and there was an opportunity to sample these vintage delights on a shuttle service between the town centre and South Parade Pier.

Another seaside call in 1961 was Gosport Ferry, where the amazing fleet of the still-independent Provincial (Gosport & Fareham) buzzed about. There were many elderly AECs, some with chassis dating back to 1931, and some still with their original bodies. The newer buses were Guy Arabs with Guy or Reading bodies, including some with Deutz air-cooled engines. Provincial had open-toppers too — I saw a utility Guy and a 1932 AEC Regent.

Left: *Paignton in 1962, and one of Devon General's MCW-bodied open-top Atlanteans, 'Sir Francis Drake'.*
Below: *Bournemouth in 1961, and a 1943 Corporation Weymann-bodied Guy Arab.*

Other elderly buses encountered on that 1961 holiday were Southdown's open-top utility Guys and Brighton Corporation's fine 1939 Weymann-bodied AEC Regents. At the time, Brighton Corporation and Brighton Hove & District buses were in attractive red and cream liveries, but since then the Corporation adopted a rather insipid blue and white livery, and BH&D buses disappeared into Southdown green. Brighton without red buses just doesn't look the same, somehow.

For all that, Brighton is a particularly fine town, and those 1939 Corporation Regents echoed much of the local elegance. Not surprisingly, one of these buses was saved for preservation, and it is interesting to note how many of these 1961 survivors have in fact been preserved; among the ranks of preserved open-toppers are a Bournemouth TD5 Titan, several Hants & Dorset Bristol K5Gs and Portsmouth Titan TD4s, and a Provincial Regent.

Of course, open-toppers need not be elderly buses. At Torquay in 1962 I came across Devon General's open-top Atlanteans, a most pleasant way of seeing the beauties of Torbay. The student conductors on these Atlanteans always seemed to have found a particularly pleasant summer job — at least when the weather was good.

Elsewhere on the south coast, I discovered Eastbourne's attractive blue and cream Borough Transport fleet in 1975, with attractions like a roofless — not topless — East Lancs-bodied Leyland Titan

PD2, and a long-lived 1950 AEC Regal III with East Lancs rear-entrance body.

There is something right about blue seaside buses. Great Yarmouth has them too — a smart fleet that was pretty varied when I first visited the resort in 1957. It had an open-topper, a cream AEC Regent/English Electric of 1934 vintage, Guy Arabs, still with wooden seats, and Weymann-bodied Leyland Titan TD5s. The newer fleet was smart, too — AEC and Leyland double-deckers with Massey bodies, and in later years these were joined by Albion Nimbuses, Daimler Freelines and Leyland Atlanteans, and more recently by AEC Swifts and Bristol VRTs.

I have been to Great Yarmouth several times, but have only once visited Southend, and then at the tail-end of the 1966 season. Southend looked as if it would appeal to my fondness for honest seaside vulgarity, and even the blue-painted Corporation buses were of interest, with gems like an ex-Birmingham Daimler CWA6 open-topper — now preserved — and Scottish-associated vehicles like 'Leyland'/Alexander Lowlanders, and ex-Glasgow Leyland Worldmasters.

On the other side of the country, on the Lancashire coast, are Southport, Lytham St Annes and Blackpool, three very different resorts which I visit at the slightest excuse.

First Southport, an elegant town with all the attractions of a popular seaside resort — funfairs, open-top buses and a pier with its own railway.

The Southport Corporation fleet, first encountered in 1967, was really smart in its red and cream colours, and included single-deck and double-deck Leyland open-toppers. The double-deckers were 1947 Titan PD2/3s, and the single-deckers were ex-Ribble 1949 Tiger PS2/5s; they were used on open-top tours — and *long* open-top tours at that. Although they covered a fair part of Southport, 100 minutes seemed just too long.

On my most recent visit to Southport there were still red and cream buses about, but the Corporation was absorbed into Merseyside PTE in 1974, and more and more green buses were in evidence. The open-toppers were still there, though — one in green and two in red. One of the red examples was a former Liverpool Corporation Atlantean, converted following an accident.

The others were forward-entrance Weymann-bodied Leyland Titan PD2/40s, and I joined one of them for Tour 29, a one-hour trip around the town, much of which was spent wondering just what would happen if its started to rain, as the clouds constantly threatened. It didn't, but I couldn't help feeling that a shorter tour, or even an open-top *service,* might be a better proposition.

Within sight of Southport, across the Ribble estuary, lies Lytham St Annes, which is to Blackpool what Frinton is to Clacton, and Hove to Brighton; the posh end, you might say.

When I first visited St Annes with my parents, the local buses were provided by Lytham St Annes

Top left: *Still going strong in 1961, a Brighton Corporation 1939 AEC Regent/Weymann outside the station.*
Centre left: *Brighton again, and a Southdown utility Guy Arab/Park Royal open-topper at Pool Valley.*
Left: *OPN-toppers? Two Bristol Lodekka LD6Bs delivered in 1959 to Brighton Hove & District, and which passed to Southdown when the two firms merged in 1969. When photographed at Devil's Dyke in 1975, OPN 801 was in Southdown green, and OPN 808 preserved in traditional BH&D red and cream.*

Right: *A veteran which was still in use at Eastbourne in 1975 was this 1950 AEC Regal III with East Lancs 32-seat rear entrance body.*

Above left: *Several of these 1938 Leyland Titan TD5s with 48-seat Weymann bodies were still in active service with Great Yarmouth Corporation in 1960.*

Above: *Now preserved, this Daimler CWA6 started life with Birmingham City Transport in 1945. It is seen here in service with Southend Corporation in 1966, by which time its Duple utility body had been heavily rebuilt to open-top form.*

Left: *In 1963, Southport Corporation bought this 1950 Leyland Tiger PS2/5 from Ribble, and converted its Burlingham body to open-top form. It is seen in 1967.*

Below: *Also at Southport in 1967, one of the attractive Weymann-bodied Leyland Titan PD2/40s bought in 1965 picks up passengers in Lord Street.*

Opposite: *Across the Ribble estuary in Blackpool, a scene at Blackpool's North Pier with 1934 'balloon' car 704 and 1935 Railcoach 611, as rebuilt in 1966 with lightweight plastic panelling and ends; it has since been further rebuilt to become one-man tram 12.*

Corporation, using a smart fleet of Leylands, including 'gearless' pre-war Lions and Titans. Now I visit St Annes with my own children, and the local buses are those of the Corporation's successor, Fylde Borough Council. Fylde operates Titan and Atlantean double-deckers and Bristol RE, Leyland Panther and Seddon RU saloons, with a small fleet of smart Leopard coaches. The Atlantean fleet includes ex-Liverpool examples bought from Merseyside PTE.

Fylde operates jointly with Blackpool Borough Transport, crossing the boundary at Starr Gate, the start of Blackpool's famous coastal tramway — still one of Britain's most pleasant transport experiences, for a variety of reasons. Blackpool's trams pander to a number of my weaknesses. Firstly, they are trams, and at times they are street trams, allowing those of us who were brought up on tramcars to rekindle old memories. Then they are seaside trams — the next best thing to an open-top bus in these circumstances; Blackpool does have its open-top 'boat' trams, but they can be difficult to find if the weather is at all variable. And most of all, Blackpool's trams have the undoubted advantage of Blackpool, surely the epitome of the English seaside resort. The town has all of the virtues I listed in the second paragraph — and I accept that to many these virtues will be interpreted as vices.

The tram ride from Starr Gate to Fleetwood is an hour's worth of social and transport variety at any time of the year. The constant stream of passengers on and off the tram can be every bit as fascinating as the summer crowds along the Golden Mile, many of whom seem determined to throw themselves under the wheels of the trams, prompted either by unfamiliarity or by the wares of Yates Wine Lodge.

The trams themselves are full of interest. There are the double-deck 'balloon' cars, these vast 94-seaters which require a conductor on each deck. Then there are the attractive single-deck Railcoaches which parade in different guises — as open 'boats', and in the case of the 1939 Brush cars, in largely unrebuilt form.

English Electric Railcoaches survive with rebuilt ends as driving cars for the twin-car sets, and totally rebuilt as one-man cars 1-13. You won't find one of the 1952 Coronation cars, the last totally new cars built for Blackpool but prematurely killed off by maintenance problems. Only one of the 25 was in evidence in August 1977, hidden away in the dusty recesses of Rigby Road depot. Also to be found in the depot were other oddments in the fleet. There were the illuminated trams, impressive by day and fantastic by night; and there was the small mixed fleet of works cars.

Blackpool's buses have always been rather overshadowed by the trams. In recent years the unflattering cream livery has been worn by Leyland PD3s and AEC Swifts, but in 1977 these were joined by East Lancs-bodied 33ft Leyland Atlanteans, and these carry a more attractive green and cream scheme.

Although Blackpool's own bus fleet is fairly standardised, the buses and coaches which crowd into the town every summer are remarkably varied. Blackpool attracts vehicles from every part of Britain, from independent, National Bus Company, Scottish Bus Group and even local authority fleets, and if you have ever wondered if coaching had a future, a trip to the Illuminations would soon provide the answer.

But the trams must be the prime attraction, and the 11-mile journey from Starr Gate to Fleetwood offers an intriguing mixture of sights, sounds and smells — though not all are directly connected with the tramway, of course.

Once the tramway has tiptoed through the trippers along the Golden Mile, the trams open up for an exhilarating ride along the railway-style reserved track. Past the short-turning trams at Bispham station, the trams swing inland through Cleveleys and past green fields and suburban gardens to reach the stretch of proper street tramway in Fleetwood.

The compleat transport enthusiast would then board the steamer to the Isle of Man, and resume his tram ride at Douglas, but so far I haven't had the chance to do this. Maybe someday . . .

Somerset
Scenes

Photographs by VIEWFINDER

Left: *When Western National relinquished its 261 service from Wellington to Wiveliscombe in 1972, Wivey Coaches at the behest of Somerset County Council took over. Wivey uses any of its fleet of modern coaches on the bus route at times; this Bedford/Plaxton negotiates the narrow lane to Langford Budville under zig-zagging telephone wires.*

Right: *An important part of any outing — somewhere to fill up. Shamrock & Rambler Leyland Leopard/Plaxton 'Dieppe', formerly a Ribble coach, pauses on its way to Cheddar Caves in Wells coach park on a hot May day.*

Below: *Taunton's St Mary Magdalene possesses a tower of fine and delicate proportions; many think likewise about the ECW body for the FLF Lodekka. You can be the judge of both.*

With the opening of the M5 right across Somerset to t'other side of Exeter (t'other side of the world to some!), journey times have been drastically shortened. National Travel South West 137 has been drastically foreshortened by the telephoto lens as it speeds its 740 run out of the picture towards Salcombe, hotly pursued by an Austin 1300.

Coaches calling at Taunton on their way west still use the old A38 between that town and the Wellington interchange where they rejoin the motorway. The successful Western Venturer (700) is a fast service to London via Bristol using motorways for much of the route. Verdant hedgerows by the Crown Inn at Rumwell with a London-bound Royal Blue Bristol RE/ECW. Royal Blue, which used to operate its own system before the advent of National Travel, has a guaranteed minimum mileage on National services.

Above: Western National kept a handful of its 5-cylinder Gardner-engined Bristol LS buses long after most other NBC companies had disposed of theirs. 1719 takes on passengers in Taunton bus station shortly before withdrawal in 1976. The destination of the bus is spelt with a 'g' on the OS map — presumably Western National couldn't fit the extra letter in. (Locals rarely pronounce the 'g' anyway!)

Right: The 208 also serves Culmhead signals station — one of those hush-hush places. A Lodekka FSF variant, in traditional livery but with National fleetnames, speeds along the wooded top of the beautiful Blackdowns returning to Taunton during 1974.

Below: Bristol Omnibus has a tradition of attaching the depot allocation code to the fleet number on its buses. WS 2627 belongs to Wells depot and is a 1965 Bristol MW. The busy street is in Street, famous for its shoes.

Western National Bristol VR 1050 vies with other traffic for the lead in a late morning rush.

Below: *What looks like a wide leafy lane is in fact the usually much busier A38. A lunchtime lull saw 2601 bound for an anonymous destination! Actually, it was Taunton — but would a stranger realise that?*

Right: *A transfer freight train from Albert Quay station, Cork to the main line station, causes a 1949 Leyland Tiger OPS3 of CIE to come to a halt. CIE built the 39-seat body.*

It's Nearly 37 Years...

Interest in Irish transport continues to grow, and JOHN PARKE looks back over nearly four decades at the changes — good and bad — that have taken place.

Reflection is reputedly good for the soul and, confronted with a request to consider aspects of the bus and coach industry in Ireland, one was more or less impelled in that direction even if there was no strong feeling over what future life had in store. As people age they become more conservative and it is impossible to avoid commenting that things are not what they were. This is certainly true as regards buses in Ireland and to start by putting the worst points first it must be said that the vehicles seldom look as smart as they used. We all know the adage about living in glass houses and practices that this should discourage and certainly the failing of which I complain is not peculiar to Ireland. One of the ironies of the unemployment level there and in the United Kingdom is the difficulty that operators have in recruiting sufficient and efficient maintenance staff. Shift work

and weekend work has no appeal and I suppose we must resign ourselves to that situation. When it comes to keeping up appearances a certain amount has to be forgiven an operator like Coras Iompair Eireann because of the substantial number of vehicles which has to be out-stationed while some that are garage-based have to be parked in the open. None of this helps and while new garages have been opened — that at Dundalk in November, 1977, is the latest example to come to mind — it will be a long time before ideal storage is available universally. If it comes to that I am not sure that the current liveries are best suited to minimising the effects of weather and minor damage.

Politically more contentious and still on the subject of appearances is the matter of destination blinds. The Celts seem to have a particularly strong feeling on the subject of placenames as shown by the Welsh penchant for daubing signposts. The Scots, so far at least, have been less demonstrative. The Irish have long acknowledged particular rights in Gaeltacht areas and buses based at Galway, for example, have had appropriate blinds for certain routes. More recently CIE has become almost too Gaelic-minded and buses

One of the Leyland Tiger TS11s ordered by the Great Southern Railways which had to await the end of the 1939-45 War before being bodied by what had now become Coras Iompair Eireann.

Upper right: *The express coach from Dublin about to leave Mullingar railway station for Ballina. In this case it is an M-class Leyland Leopard provincial bus, in red and cream livery.*
Lower right: *Another M-class Leopard, this time in cream and green, at Cahircaveen on the route from Killarney (Cill Airne) — the most westerly bus in Europe!*

and coaches operate often with destinations in Gaelic only. They share with British vehicles the lamentable trend towards reduced blind displays and outside the Dublin area lack even the mitigating display of a route number. It must be admitted that the CIE provincial bus timetable does set out the English, or, to be more accurate, the generally-used version of what actually appears on the blind but it can take quite a long time to work one's way through this as the translation is not immediately obvious and it is not uninteresting that a few names which appeared formerly in Gaelic — sometimes for a number of years — have reverted to the English version. Ireland counts tourists as one of its major industries and the other areas of the British Isles seem to be heading towards the same attitude. There was an admitted decline in tourism due to the unsettled state of some areas. 1977 saw a considerable improvement and when this article was being prepared the hopes for 1978 were bright, but I do wonder why so much trouble has been taken seemingly to add to complications for the visitor and, indeed, for quite a high proportion of the residents.

Turning to other aspects of change it is generally possible to be more cheerful. Pruning of bus services has been for the most part less drastic than in Britain, although in Northern Ireland the cuts have been more severe. In fairness to Ulsterbus it must be added that it has striven to be as reasonable as it can and the

efficacy of its policy has been such that it has made a profit despite its difficult operating circumstances at a time when most British operators would have given their eye teeth to do the same. How it has been achieved in the face of unending losses of vehicles through civil unrest will, it may be hoped, be told when circumstances allow.

The chief differences from the old days so far as CIE is concerned must be the now widespread adoption of one-man operation and the growth of the Expressway network of limited stop services. The former became an urgent need as the financial state of the undertaking worsened and much encouragement may be derived from the way in which it proved possible to spread omo with the support of the staff. The one qualification that must be made concerns the Dublin City area where the staff has remained short-sightedly adamant. One could wish it possible to hope that there will have been a change in circumstances by the time these words are read but this would be extreme optimism. It follows from all this that there has been a tendency to go slow on major bus changes in the city services and many of the routes are much the same as they were 20 years ago — 30 years ago there were of course still some trams although they had dwindled to two main routes and the then-Great Northern Hill of Howth operation.

Growth of Greater Dublin in population and in

A Leyland-bodied Royal Tiger coach demonstrator beside one of the Great Northern Railways AEC Regal IIIs in the bus station at Dundalk.

Right: An E-class Leyland Leopard and one of the Van Hool-McArdle bodied Atlanteans, both in buttermilk livery, on stands in Lower Gardiner Street used by Dublin City services.

industry, mostly of the lighter kinds, has been marked and many of the bus developments have taken the form of extensions of routes to serve new suburb housing areas. The newer estates, at least, are blessed with roads reasonably suitable for services although there seems to have been a singular succession of cases where dilatoriness in completing new road works or making short but essential improvements to existing thoroughfares has set back by years the prospects of much-needed new links. Oddly enough this has applied more in northern areas of the city than in the south. The northern counterpart of the useful southern circumferential route 17 from Blackrock to Dolphins Barn via Churchtown, Terenure and Crumlin is very much an infant-in-arms by comparison. Numbered 17A it plies between Kilbarrack and Finglas via Coolock, Kilmore, Santry and Ballymun and has now attained as many weekday journeys and more on Sunday than its elder. Closer in, but still semi-circular in character, the 18 which starts at Sandymount and worked for many years to Kenilworth Park by way of Ballsbridge, Ranelagh and Rathmines, found itself extended to the very large housing area at Ballyfermot and has more recently stretched further north-westwards to Palmerstown, another developing area where, incidentally, Van Hool McArdle indicated some two years ago that it planned to build its new works.

The introduction of more one-way schemes has led over the years to a good many changes in the city centre terminals of routes and it may be this that influenced the adoption of 'An Lar' as the display on inbound routes other than cross-city ones. The words mean roughly speaking city centre but in no way indicate that you will finish up particularly close to all the others and a walk from Lower Gardiner Street to say College Green could be quite daunting to some. Habits are hard to discard but I must admit to continuing to find it odd that Dalkey bus leaves from Eden Quay particularly after always having caught the tram from the now vanished Nelson Pillar and indeed the replacing bus, while rectitude is still further hampered by still, in memory, associating Eden Quay more with the dark blue of the Great Northern buses for Howth or Swords. The provincial buses vanished from Aston Quay a long time ago now, but the permutations which have since been made on its use as a terminus by city routes are so numerous that I will not try to set them down.

Mention just now of the provincial services brings one inevitably to Busaras, the bus station in Store Street which was surrounded by so much controversy before it was built, let alone opened. Looking back, I have no doubt that it was justified and I am glad to have had a part, even a small one, in the battle for it. Now, however, there are grounds for those who argue

that its adequacy has diminished. Its area for vehicles is insufficient for the peak departure periods even though it is relatively quiet for some hours in each day. Its use too for picking up and setting down passengers on day and extended tours can moreover complicate the issue if these, unavoidably, conflict with the peak. A further factor has been the advent of the Expressway services since these are additional for the most part rather than replacements of the existing trunk routes.

The Expressway services are, however, by no means concerned only with Dublin and their purpose is more to provide convenient cross-country links. These have in some instances replaced rail facilities such as those southward from Ballina to Limerick via Claremorris, Athenry and Ennis where the road journey takes 4hr 50min which may be compared with roundly 4hr by train. The finishing touches have yet to be put to the network and some adjustments have already been made. Much of the development has taken place in the past three years and figures issued late in 1977 showed that there had been an average increase of 13.5 per cent in passenger traffic so that travellers on express buses were expected to total nearly 600,000 in the year. There had been a twenty per cent rise on the Galway-Dundalk service via Loughrea, Ballinasloe, Athlone, Moate, Mullingar, Athboy, Navan and Drogheda which, incidentally,

makes train connections to and from Belfast at Dundalk. There is also one of the older services, worked jointly with Ulsterbus, between Galway and Belfast via Roscommon, Longford, Clones, Monaghan, Armagh and Portadown. Other joint routes are Dublin-Derry and the slightly younger Dublin-Coleraine with a summer extension to Portrush. The latter had a twenty-five per cent traffic increase in 1977!

Although it is not a major trunk route in the way that many of the others are, I feel that reference should be made to the summer service between Galway and Cork via West Clare and the Shannon ferry. This operates on weekdays via Kinvara, Ballyvaughan, Lisdoonvarna, Ennistymon, Lahinch, Miltown Malbay, Kilkee, Kilrush, Ballybunion, Listowel, Tralee, Killarney and Macroom and takes approximately 8¼hr compared with the 4hr of the service through Limerick. I must admit that I have yet to make the journey but the added bonus of traversing the territory of the West Clare Railway beloved of Percy French and the route of the Listowel & Ballybunion — would that I had seen it — makes the whole idea very attractive. I wish only that the northbound journey was due in Galway earlier in the evening. It seems that the further developments which I mentioned earlier may well affect particularly the Midlands area. Routes such as that from Sligo to Cork

Photographed in 1965, a Saro-bodied Leyland Tiger Cub, ex-East Midland, of County Donegal Railways Joint Committee seen at Lifford border post.

via Boyle, Roscommon, Athlone, Birr, Roscrea, Thurles, Cashel, Cahir and Fermoy, with an ingenious connection at Roscrea with the Dublin-Limerick Expressway coach have promised well and an interesting seasonal exercise is the operation from Galway to Wexford with Rosslare extension for ferry connections when appropriate.

It may be hoped that the foregoing has been encouraging but, before the complaint is levelled as to lack of mention of independent operators, I should add that their lot has certainly improved in the past 37 years even if there have been some notable failures in the process due mostly to excessive zeal. Stage service operations have not changed all that much but one certainly notices the great increase that there has been in the number of coaches to be seen on private hire work and, over much of the year, party charter work for inclusive tours operators. The growth in this business has undoubtedly led to the expansion of many businesses to quite substantial sizes and also to the buying of larger and sometimes heavier types of coach. There is still a tendency to buy secondhand from dealers or operators in the United Kingdom but the availability in the country of Van Hool McArdle and of Asco has had its effect in the appearance of new Fords and Bedfords in some profusion especially with Jackson's of Cavan and Crosson of Drogheda as main dealers, apart from their significant role as operators. The latter firm is also one of the dozen or so members of the Eirebus organisation which is now

some seven years old and has a fleet of 30 first line coaches and a further 20 in support plus 40 or thereabouts other psvs. Some of these are buses — five of the group have stage services — and many of the rest are used mainly on the schools services which have had a great effect upon Irish psv operation. CIE itself is responsible for the maintenance of a large fleet of buses amd minibuses in special livery, many of them manned by part-time staff, and the independent operators meet most of the other needs. Reference should also be made to the rather confused situation in County Donegal which is almost cut off from the rest of the Republic and has produced in recent years quite a bunch of small operators who seem to be something of a law unto themselves. To an observer even identification of owners can often prove difficult if not impossible. Many have developed weekend services linking the county with South-West Scotland and have also established links with operators across the North Channel. When this article was being prepared there were rumours that 'something was going to be done' about the situation. Certainly established operators have been hit by the competition and this includes the Londonderry & Lough Swilly Railway which has been experiencing hard times with the pressures on cross-border traffic.

There have been changes and more must come, be they for better or for worse. From nearly 37 years' personal ecquaintance I feel able to aver that Ireland continues to grow in psv interest.

What is the attraction of half-cab buses?

If this question is to be answered, we have to start off by assuming that buses — or at least some sorts of buses — are attractive anyway; it would take too long to discuss the basic fact of whether buses can be attractive at all (especially in the face of such competition as trams, trains, girls, alcohol, the English countryside in autumn, the operas of Bellini, etc, etc...)

So, assuming that there can be some attraction about buses, I realise that certain stand out from the common herd, and if I pause to consider Buses I Have Known over the past thirty years (before which time I was too young to know anything about them) the ones which have appealed to me most are Paris open-back buses, three-axle buses, and half-cab buses.

The charm of Paris buses is, I would imagine, fairly obvious, besides which I have written of it before so will refrain from further eulogies. Three-axle buses have always been sufficiently rare and sufficiently large to create an impression. But half-cab buses are, or until not so long ago *were*, pretty thick on the ground. Therefore I have to consider Half-Cab Buses I Have Known, and see if I can discover *what there is about them* ...

I was brought up on a mixture of King Alfred of Winchester, Royal Blue, and Hants & Dorset. In my schooldays I was taken after church on Sundays to Winchester coach station, which was conveniently close to the church, to have an ice-cream. Was this a compensation for the boredom of the sermon, a bribe to ensure willing attendance the following Sunday? Perhaps the slight profanity of these occasions lent glamour to the coaches. The ones which impressed me most, presumably because there was nearly always one there, were the Royal Blue half-cab Bristols with luggage rack on the roof and four destination blinds above the saloon. Other coaches didn't linger so much in the memory. Nor was there anything special about the new generation of full-fronted Royal Blues, not even the vehicle which was alleged to have carried Mitchell the Murderer on his escape. The old Royal Blues had more character. They were very vehemently one-sided, seemingly more so than other half-cabs... and perhaps one-sidedness is a chief cause of the attraction, the appeal of peculiarity. You expect a motor vehicle to be even across the front simply because this nearly always is the case...

Full-fronted buses were at this time edging into the ranks of King Alfred's single-deckers as well as

THE ALLURE OF THE HALF-CAB

ROBERT E. JOWITT

A Lisbon AEC Regal starts out from a traffic jam with a fine cloud of exhaust.

into the Royal Blue, but the double-deckers were all still half-cabs, and I regarded them as perfectly normal and every-day. Their charm now, I must admit, lies in the fact that they are yesterday, shades of lost youth.

More or less the same applies to Hants & Dorset buses. The only H & D bus for which I had any affection was 1145, and that merely because I saw one of my first girl friends home on it. (Mary, Mary, where are you now, twenty years later?) The H & D half-cabs still running today have for me no appeal except that of age.

Age definitely adds charm to a bus, and in the late 1950s and early 1960s there were a lot of buses which were then pretty old — and would now be pearls beyond price — working out their last days as showmen's transport. And they were all half-cabs. But was it the aura of the fairground, the smell of chips and hot dogs, the blaring of Buddy Holly from the dodgems, the girls in just-above-the-knee skirts vastly fluffed out with stiff petticoats, which gave a magic to this venerable fleet and thus added more allure to the half-cab?

No, it can't have been just the fairground ...

Age counted too, for buses then

Above: *An AEC and a girl with winkle-pickers in a Bradford fog in 1965.*

Below: *A Western National Bristol at Sennen Cove, Cornwall, in 1965.*

Above right: *A morose-looking Crossley in Ashton-under-Lyne in 1964, is in good company with a scowling Bristol in Pontypridd in 1962 (right).*

still active, and increased the merits of, for example, the AECs at Douglas, Isle of Man, and Gosport (Provincial), and the wartime Utility Guy Arab in Bournemouth, all of which were running when I was a photography student — more interested in photographing buses than sundry useless objects the lecturers thought fit to set before our lenses . . . The Bournemouth Guy Arab was notable not just by antiquity but also because nearly all the other Bournemouth vehicles at the time were smoothly full-fronted. A utility half-cab is noticably angular.

But is may be argued that newer Guy Arabs weren't at all bad. East Kent had some nice ones from the early 1950s, and they looked very smart in their dark red and cream as they squeezed through the city gate at Canterbury.

In fact certain half-cabs which I cannot count as old — because I remember them as brand new — are rather splendid, especially the AECs (Bridgemasters, Regal Vs or Renowns) of Southampton, Eastbourne, Bradford, Leicester, King Alfred and elsewhere. As I deem these buses new it can't be age which sways me in their favour; it must be their handsome appearance. Though they have the innate half-cab lopsidedness they are definitely good-looking.

But strange looking half-cabs are not to be ignored. Perhaps they don't seem strange to the inhabitants in their own districts, but whereas the above-mentioned AECs all look very much alike, a stranger to Birmingham finds the traditional Brum type half-cab double-decker quite unique to that city, quite unlike any buses elsewhere. Similarly a 'foreigner' in Lancashire finds the expression on the faces of the Crossleys very morose and forbidding. And I remember a particularly scowling bus I once encountered in Pontypridd. Barring that it had a Bristol radiator it was like nothing I've seen before or since.

These local variations are very fascinating, but are not the answer to the question of half-cabs, for oddity excludes the normal, and I must quote two cases of normal half-cabs, one rural, the other

73

Below: *A Crossley of typical Birmingham appearance surrounded by impressive architecture in the city centre in 1965.*
Opposite: *Burgos left-hand drive Pegaso with the Cathedral in the background.*

PORTLAND ROAD 7

JOJ 378

thoroughly urban, with particular allure.

I have mentioned rather disparagingly the Hants & Dorset buses, and ought therefore to speak in the same terms of the Eastern National, Western National, and others with similar buses. But I conceived a great affection for the very ordinary little Western National Bristol which ran the service to Sennon Cove in Cornwall when I spent a holiday there. I liked the way it pushed busily along the road by the beach. The air of romance, however, was perhaps created by brilliant sunsets and once by the presence of a shark swimming in the sea only a couple of hundred yards from the shore and the bus. The bus itself was nothing outstanding.

The other case is London. You might describe RTs and RMs as local types of buses like the Birmingham ones, but they are world-famous and probably more typical a symbol of London than any of the other symbols of London (and they serve all the other symbols of London, anyway). The faces of the RT and RM are the archetype of all half-cab faces. Very British.

So we take our passports and travel abroad, to see a little of what the Continent can offer in the way of half-cabs.

The French had a sprinkling in the 1930s, but after the war went in for full fronts. Aa a consequence, *demi-cabines* must have been very few and far between by the time I first visited France, and I saw only one, a local pirate in Clermont Ferrand in 1960. Here was age (it was nearly falling to pieces), rarity (perhaps the only half-cab left in France) and foreign flavour (French) to render it magic, and I have to wonder whether its delight lay in the fact that it was a *French* half-cab with the half-cab on the *wrong side*, rather than simply because it was a half-cab.

The question of the cab being on the wrong side (the right side as you look at the front of the bus, the left when you're inside) needs further consideration . . .

Lisbon abounds in AECs which might be exactly of the Bradford-Eastbourne-Leicester type were it

not that they are completely mirror-image. There are also various sorts of single-deckers, and some old Regal double-deckers. Among the latter are buses with no rear platform doors; I found it really disconcerting to board the platform on the wrong side and mount stairs which turned right instead of left . . . But all these buses are really nothing but British buses built to cater for foreign tastes, and can claim no more half-cab merit than their British counterparts except in their wrong-handedness. Lisbon anyhow is full of very symmetrical and very old trams which are far more beautiful than even the best half-cabs.

But if we stay in the Iberian peninsula we may come nearer to finding the reason for the allure of the half-cab . . .

Burgos in Spain is very famous for its noble Cathedral. I visited the Cathedral in a torrential downpour. The roof was leaking in many places. I retired to a café, waiting for the cloudburst to stop so that I could photograph buses. While I was in the café all the lights went out, and as, a few minutes later, water started to drop from one of the light bulb sockets, I wasn't really surprised . . .

When the rain finally ceased I went out and looked at the buses. They were indigenous Spanish buses, built by Pegaso, the Spanish lorry builders.

And they were half-cabs.

And some of them had cabs on the left, the Spanish side, and some of them had cabs on the right side . . .

Although they were very ugly, very bashed-up, and painted in a rather miserable blue and grey, they constituted quite the most fascinating half-cab operation I have beheld . . . I suppose just because you never knew if the next one would have its cab on the left or on the right.

Which goes nearer than anything else towards proving (nearer than Sunday ice-cream or the fluffed out skirts of 1960 fairground girls or the traditional Olde Englishe Charme of an RT in Oxford Street) that the allure of the half-cab really does lie in the fact that it is uneven, odd, eccentric. And surely there is a fascination in eccentricity . . .

75

The Morris Eight

Photographs by DON MORRIS

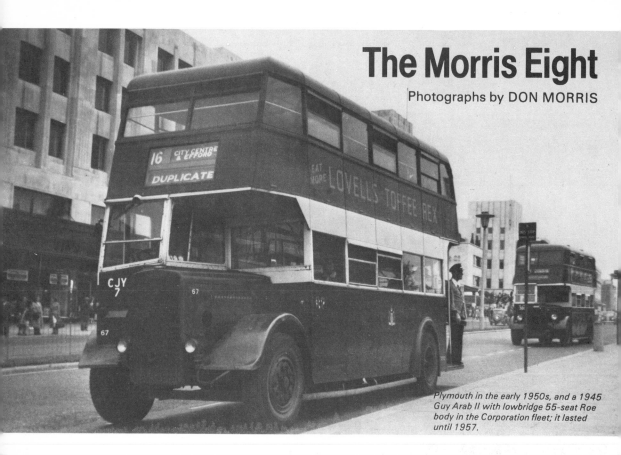

Plymouth in the early 1950s, and a 1945 Guy Arab II with lowbridge 55-seat Roe body in the Corporation fleet; it lasted until 1957.

An earlier utility Guy Arab, a 1942 Sunderland Corporation example with prewar style Roe 48-seat centre entrance body.

A wartime delivery to Birmingham City Transport, a Daimler COG6 with 8ft wide MCW 56-seat body. It was built for service in Johannesburg, but the hostilities prevented its export.

Photographed in its home town when new in 1954, a Walsall Corporation Daimler CLG5 with Northern Counties 60-seat body.

Halifax Corporation had six of these
Daimler CD650s with 56-seat bodies,
delivered in 1951.

A late survivor of AEC's unusual
side-engined Q model, Grimsby
Corporation 48 with 56-seat centre
entrance Roe body. Its original petrol
engine was replaced by an AEC 7.7 litre
diesel in 1943.

An early postwar delivery for Liverpool Corporation, a 1945 AEC Regent II with Weymann/Liverpool body.

Delivered to Cardiff Corporation in 1946, a utility-style Bristol K6A with Park Royal 56-seat body.

Door-to-Door Service

To help a serious vehicle shortage in 1948-50, Bristol double-deckers destined for BTC fleets were diverted to London Transport. This 1949 Brighton Hove & District K5G with ECW body takes on passengers in York Road, Waterloo, while working the 76 route.

MICHAEL DRYHURST remembers the buses and the bus routes that have passed the various homes in which he has lived, in Britain and overseas.

Shepperton-on-Thames is a name now familiar to all readers of Ian Allan books, but in 1939 its only claim to fame was the Sound City film studios. And the fact that my family moved there that year!

At the time of our move, Shepperton was served by two London Transport bus routes, 218: Kingston - Esher - Walton - Shepperton - Laleham - Staines, and 237: Hounslow - Feltham - Sunbury - Shepperton - Chertsey. Then, as now, the routes were worked by Kingston and Hounslow respectively, although the buses used have changed somewhat.

My earliest recollections go back to about 1942. The 218 was worked with single-deck T-type buses, of various sub-types, the most common being the ex-General 1T1 and ex-Tilling versions, these being petrol-engined AEC Regal I 662 chassis. The ex-General buses were originally rear entrance, having been converted to front entrance before the War, but as I graded buses in those days by their appearance (which had to be friendly) the ex-General Ts did not

fare too well in my top twenty, as the roof overhang above the cab tended to make them look rather bad-tempered, whereas the wide destination boxes fore and aft on the former Tilling buses gave them a friendly look. The General Ts also lost out on the Dryhurst popularity stakes by not sporting rear destination boxes — instead they had a rather grotty route stencil in the bottom of the emergency exit window. Other buses that occasionally turned up on 218 were ex-Green Line Ts of 1930, and those Ts that carried 1935 Weymann bodies, originally mounted on rebodied AEC Reliance chassis; the ex-Green Line jobs had frowning cabs, and so didn't make the Dryhurst charts, but the Weymann-bodied jobs looked happy, and were definitely top twenty material.

Turning to 237, I can just about recall the 20-seat Leyland Cubs that were on this route when we first moved to Shepperton, probably because it was this route which actually passed our front door. However, around 1942/3 these one-man-operated buses were replaced by AEC Renown single-deckers of the LT class, more familiarly known as 'Scooters', which were 35-seaters, the body being merely a longer version of the General T, and so suffered from the same bad-tempered look at the front, although some of the Scooters did make up for this by having rear

80

destination boxes. Actually, I am as bemused now as I was then, by the fact that some buses of the LTL (single-deck LT) type had rear screens, and others did not. We lived by Shepperton Square, and I can still hear those petrol-engined LTs back-firing as the drivers changed down to take the bend by the Anchor Garage.

Wartime was with us in those days, and the War manifested itself on the transport scene in a number of ways. The London Transport single-deckers all had transverse seating to increase their capacity, and I recall that they took as many standing passengers as could be crammed into the bus — probably an exaggeration, but that is how it appeared to a four-year old boy. Wartime restrictions meant that we did not have bus services until after midday on Sundays, and it also meant that we got bus stops. Previously, in London Transport's outer suburban area, there had not been bus stops, the vehicles stopping where and when hailed, but as this was felt to be wasteful of fuel it was decided to regularise stopping places. I was very put out when I discovered that the faceless ones of 55 Broadway had decided that my local stop was only of sufficient importance to merit 'request' status!

Although out of Central London, one was very much aware of the War whilst living in Shepperton. The Luftwaffe made monotonously regular attacks on the Vickers works, across the river at Weybridge, and I can recall vividly watching Sound City Studios going up in flames, after an attack by incendiary bombs. And then there was all that anti-splinter mesh on the passenger windows of buses, with a diamond-shaped cutout in the centre, to let you see where you were... By the time you had adjusted your height to look through the little diamond window, the bus had passed your stop anyway! Underground cars also had the anti-splinter mesh, and if you look at older Underground car windows, you can see the pattern of the mesh left by the adhesive.

The variety of buses in the London fleet in those days is incredible to recall, and even in localised areas, there were many different buses to see, as can be demonstrated taking a very quick ride on the two Shepperton routes.

As now, the Kingston terminus then of 218 was Kingston bus station, which is part of Kingston Garage. I think everything terminating in Kingston used the bus station in those days, although I cannot recall any of the Country Area routes in Kingston, so maybe the open space by the railway station was in use then? Anyway, as we board our 218, we are surrounded by Scooters on 201, 213, 215, 216 and 219, those on 219 being painted grey, as camouflage for working to Vickers at Weybridge. On one side of the bus station is an RT2 on 85 to Putney, and a standard ST on 131 to Walton via Molesey. At that time the RT2s came second in my top twenty, mainly because I was a top-box lover, and the first 151 RTs sported these at back and front (except for RT 110), and I thought the standard STs were cheerful-looking, so they figured quite high in my charts. As we wait to pull out into the traffic, a 60-seater ex-LGOC STL goes by on 65, which I quite liked, despite their cab overhang; the other STLs on 65, the so-called 'leaning back' version, were not Dryhurst favourites. Past the Kingston Empire (now a supermarket) and down to the lights by the Elite cinema, now a clothing store. Behind us a vehicle silently glides to a halt. It is a class A1 trolleybus, affectionately known as a 'Diddler', on the 603 route, one of 60 such trolleybuses (of classes A1 and A2) that passed to the LPTB from London United; these were 6-wheeled AEC 663T chassis with 56-seat Union Construction bodies, very reminiscent of the UCC 'Feltham' tramcars. We move along Portsmouth Road, in company with 201, 215 and 219 and at The Dittons, we meet another Diddler, laying over on 602. The 201 branches off right here, and the next route that we meet is 152, at the Scilly Isles roundabout, working between Mitcham and Hampton Court Station; my earliest recollection of the buses on this route is of Daimler utilities. Also at this point we encounter 72, running between East Acton and Esher with RT2s, and we trundle along behind one of these handsome buses until it turns round in the forecourt of a pub in Esher High Street, nowadays occupied by a supermarket. We also meet 206 and 416 here, but I cannot for the life of me remember what buses worked on these routes then. We and 219 turn off right here, leaving 215 to go on along the A3, whilst 219 leaves us shortly, at Hersham Green.

The next buses we encounter are at Halfway, Walton, where we meet the Dennis Aces of Walton-on-Thames Motor Co, who work a service between Walton Bridge and Walton station, and I feel that they were then probably the only independent bus operator working wholly within the London Transport Central Area. Further on, and we come to the Capitol Cinema (now the Odeon), Walton, which is the terminus for Country routes 461 and 461A, the former sporting STLs with lowbridge LPTB bodies, whilst forward-entrance STLs were usually to be found on 461A, and farther up the High Street we see STs on 131, at the T-junction of Church Street with Bridge Street and High Street. This is a crossroads these days! On our own now, over Walton Bridge, until we meet the Scooters on 237; we travel along Green Lane with them, to Shepperton Station. No imposing Ian Allan offices here — just a small shack on that site, housing an estate agent! The 237 turns left into the High Street, and we head down Laleham Road, on our own now until Staines, where we meet the most beauteous buses of all time — 'top box' STLs. I could write reams on these super-looking buses, suffice to say here that we were looking at them on 90, in red livery, and on 441 in green. We can see STs on 116/117, Scooters on 216, and lowbridge STLs on 461 and 436, with assorted Ts on 462, but wrack my brains as much as I can, I don't recall what other buses were to be seen on the remaining Country routes. If we take a 436, 461 or 462 from Staines to Chertsey, we can pick up our Scooter on 237.

At one time, General double-deckers had worked through Shepperton to Chertsey, on the 90 route, but this had subsequently become single-deck 137, to be renumbered 237. We pull out of the railway station forecourt into Guildford Street, as an Aldershot & District Dennis Lancet passes us on 48 to Guildford, 48A to Camberley also serving Chertsey. Down to the lights, where we travel along the main shopping area in company with 436, 461 and 462, and then at the Town Hall, we leave them and turn right to head for Shepperton, thence to Lower Sunbury, where we are joined by more Scooters, on 216, which run with us to Sunbury Clock, where we meet those smiling STLs on the 90. Straight across here, and heading for Lower Feltham, during the course of which we traverse a section of Vicarage Road that is yet to receive a tarmac dressing, and then we are running alongside STs on 117. At Feltham Station we meet more STLs, on the 90B, and more Scooters on the 201, although this route is soon to be cut back to Hampton Court, to be replaced by an extension of 152. In Bedfont Road we work alongside both 116 and 117 with STs, and at Hounslow Heath further STLs, this time on the 120 route from Hanwell garage. Further along we come to the specially-constructed turning circle that is the terminus of the 657 trolleybus route, at Wellington Road. Hounslow (later to become Isleworth) provides C1-class AECs with Weymann bodies for this route. At The Bell, we sight another ST-worked route, the 81, and then further STs on 33, 110 and 111, and RTs on 37. Nunhead used to use LT double-deckers on 37, but I don't ever recall seeing them at Hounslow — which does not mean to say that they didn't go there. However, Hounslow did not boast a bus station in those days, so that you are turfed-off your 237 at the London Road entrance to the garage, whereupon the bus disappears inside to lay-over, subsequently reappearing into Kingsley Road, to pick-up passengers, who have had to brave all weathers at the unsheltered stops. However, uncomfortable as it was in those days, waiting for a bus there, Hounslow rated three crossed double-deckers in my top termini competition because its RTs and STs were nice, but it took on a new dimension on Sundays when some nice

bloke at 55 Broadway deemed the 27 route would operate ('tween Hounslow and Highgate) — with a healthy sprinkling of top-box STLs. Oh, bliss! But even my young brain was bemused by the Sundays-only service being numbered 27, whereas the daily operation was the 27A... But then, the same situation exists today, with the 40 and 40A.

But enough of this rambling.

By 1944, by which time I had attained the grand age of six, I must have become intolerable to my parents, because at that tender age I was bundled off to boarding school, at St Albans, with the parental excuse that the bombing was less heavy there than it was in the Shepperton area. And I bought that — until the first night at school, when a doodle-bug cut out directly above the dormitory.

But, somebody, somewhere, loved me, because top box STLs ran past the door.

These were on the long Luton to Uxbridge 321 route, and that same someone had been very thoughtful and arranged to have a stop sited opposite the school, so that I was able to admire my beauties, from the dormitory windows. Other routes past the door were 315, St Albans to Garston, and 355, to Boreham Wood. The 315 presented me with a new type of double-decker. I was familiar with the 'Bluebird' LTs that worked in Central London, but here was that same body on a four-wheeled chassis, and classed as an ST. They got well into my top twenty, which is more than can be said for the 4Q4 single-deckers on 355. These side-engined buses had Birmingham Railway Carriage & Wagon Co bodies, with the roofline gently sloping from the full-front cab down to the rear dome, and this, combined with the single-rear wheels, extremely short rear overhang and swept-out, flared rear panels reminded me of a Pekinese dog. And I didn't like Pekinese dogs. However, the STLs on 321 made up for bed by 7pm, cod-liver oil, burnt custard and drowned cabbage!

Other buses in St Albans that I remember from those days were forward-entrance STLs, usually on the 354 Fleetville circular, green standard and leaning back STLs, standard STs (some with square dash, that were new to me, but ex-National), ex-Green Line Ts of 1930/1, the Weymann rebodied Ts (which got good placings in the Dryhurst top twenty by virtue of their smiling windscreens) and 'leaning back' and 60-seat STLs on Central Area route 84, which moved into the top twenty on Sundays when it was extended from Arnos Grove to Walthamstow, and Palmers Green came on to the route with the top box cuties.

Apart from the variety of vehicles in those days, London liveries were also interesting. The standard Central livery was red, with white window surrounds, brown roofs and red oxide wheels, but difficulty with

Heading via Shepperton for Staines, London Transport AEC Regal T2 picks up in Eden Street, Kingston. Built in 1929, this 1948 view shows the bus still fitted with wartime perimeter seating.

The T class, mainstay of the 218 route, were the former LGOC buses plus the ex-Thomas Tilling Regals, as exemplified by T312, a 1932 bus with Tilling 28-seat body. These buses were basically a single-deck version of the Tilling ST, and were readily distinguishable by the wide destination boxes, front and rear. T213 is at New Malden on the 213 route.

The ex-Green Line T types were also familiar in the Shepperton area. This is T359, on loan to Hounslow.

83

paint supplies meant that many buses were brown, or red oxide, instead of red, and many of the utility Guys being then delivered came in all-over grey. Country area buses were to the same basic standard livery, albeit green instead of red, whilst a number of STs and STLs at St Albans had light green window surrounds, a legacy of prewar days.

In March 1946 I got mumps, and they put me in solitary. Well, not exactly, but in a dormitory by myself. I relieved the boredom by looking out of the window at the traffic, and I was doing this one afternoon when I nearly fell clean out. There was an 84 standing at the traffic lights at the top of Holywell Hill, a leaning-back STL painted all-over in red, with a cream band 'tween decks, and another small cream band on the beading above the upper deck windows. It looked like no other London bus that I had ever seen, and was, of course, the forerunner of the postwar livery of cream cantrail and cream upper deck window surrounds. But I was so transfixed by the sight of this shiny red livery that I didn't hear Matron's approach, being only aware of her presence when she slammed the window on to my waist and proceeded to thump my buttocks with a slipper, whilst the top half of me was helpless to do anything but scream!

Shortly after this, more treats came, with some strange double-deckers on the 321, in both red and green liveries. These were the 18STL20 variant, standard crash gearbox AEC Regent II chassis with 7.7-litre engines and provincial Weymann bodywork. They got 8 out of 10, losing two points for being top-box-less. Another surprise was seeing a 4Q4 on the 355 with a dark green roof — better than the brown, but they were still four-wheeled Pekinese as far as I was concerned! And the 315 became the 351.

In August 1946 I left boarding school, and that final journey home to Shepperton was different.

Hitherto we had journeyed twixt home and school via 237 to Hounslow, the Picadilly Line thence to Arnos Grove, and then an 84 to St Albans. This time, my mother was very secretive (maybe she didn't want the World to know I was 'out'?), and booked only as far as Barnet Church on 84, where she sprang her surprise — my first-ever ride on a Green Line coach! These limited stop services were newly-reintroduced after wartime suspension, and we caught a 716, which was a 10T10 type AEC Regal I 0661, with 8.8-litre engine and Chiswick-built front entrance body, the only single-decker to get 10 out of 10. Well, couldn't fail, could it? STL-stype windscreen, handsome destination boxes rear and aft, radiused windows, wheel discs front and rear, and a very pleasant engine note... Mind you, my inaugural Green Line trip could have been happier. Mother booked from Barnet to Kingston, at which point we were to take the train to Shepperton, and not being then too familiar with Green Line routes, it was sometime before I realised the 716 went to Walton, and I made it quite plain in a somewhat vociferous way that I was at a loss to understand why we could not stay on the beautiful 10T10 until Walton and change there on to the 218. A sharp clip around the ear'ole convinced me of the superiority of the Southern Electric.

Back home in Sheppeton my local route, the 237, was still worked with Scooters, although the 218 had some new buses. These were the 14T12 AEC Regals, really a single-deck version of the 18STL20s that were on 321; these new buses had not a vestige of the London look about them, but they sported a nice new red livery — all-over red, with cream relief on the beading above and below the windows. They had rather a mean windscreen, together with a drooping destination box, but their handsome, long, AEC radiators, front wings and 'cheerful' back window got them well placed in the charts.

The severity of the winter of 1946/7 was such that my mother's health was affected, and doctors felt that we should leave the dampness of the Thames Valley and move to an area with a more bracing climate. My father had a meeting with himself, and so we moved to Brighton.

After four months, I ran away, back to Shepperton.

Well, I mean to say, it was bad enough to be somewhere that didn't boast top box STLs, but four-wheeled trolleybuses, rear-entrance single-deckers, no *Picture Post* eyes by the destination box and buses that chugged... These were called 'Bristols'.

Well, they came and got me back, and after a while I found that there were some familiar sights and sounds, that linked Brighton buses to their — what I considered to be superior — London brothers. Brighton Corporation buses ran past our Preston Road house, on the 35A route, and their Nos 60-80 were very similar to the LT 18STL20s, albeit dating from 1939, but better still, their engine note was very similar to that of the standard STL, so they became very firm friends, to such an extent that when they were withdrawn, I bought one. Brighton Corporation also had some new Regent IIIs which were 'friends', because I had watched them being bodied at Weymann's Addlestone Works, which was but a short bike ride from my former home at Shepperton.

But Brighton, Hove & District's buses took some getting used to, although they had familiar faces too, in the shape of 1931 AEC Regents with Tilling or Dodson open-staircase bodies, that were the same as the ex-Tilling STs owned by London Transport and which Hounslow garage was using as extras on 116 and 117 at that time. I was not too well acquainted with London Transport's utility Bristols, having only

The writer's all-time favourite, the London STL with roof-box body. STL2383 heads west along Marylebone Road, past Baker Street station.

seen them from a Piccadilly Line train when they were laying-over at Northfields station on 97, but I was able to recognise the fact that BH&D 6366-75 were Bristols with Park Royal bodies virtually the same as LT B1-9. Brighton, Hove & District was still a Tilling subsidiary in those days, the legal panel of the buses showing 'Chesterfield House, 15 Curzon Street, London, W1' was the company's registered office; the Hove address did not appear thereon until the takeover by the British Transport Commission. However, five BH&D-operated routes ran past our house, 5, 5B, 15, 15B and 35, with 5/5B worked by the Company's newest buses, 6376-6385, the first eight being K5G Bristols, 6384/5 being K6Bs; the first six of these buses had square, Tilling-style, sliding ventilators to the main windows, whereas 6382 onwards had the now-familiar ECW type. Sharing the 5/5B workings were 1939/40 Bristol K5Gs in the batch 6348-62 with assorted CAP registrations, whilst 15 was mostly worked with AEC Regents with Tilling bodies that had been rebuilt by ECW, and ECOC-bodied G05G Bristols; the 15B was the same, except for K6A utility 6373 and new K5G 6381. An interesting point is the fact that for many years, right up to absorption by Southdown, BH&D buses always worked the same duties, on the same routes, and drivers always had the same bus. The 35 route was mostly worked with 1930/1 AEC Regents that had received new Beadle or ECW bodies, and mostly converted from AEC petrol engines to Gardner 5LW units. It was ages before I could deduce why some AECs sounded like Bristols — the 5LW has a lot to answer for.

In fact, in those days, one had to deduce most things. It was still a while before *Buses Illustrated* was to appear, and if my memory serves me correctly, the only Ian Allan bus book published by 1947 was the *ABC of London Transport Services*, which came out in 1944. This talked about TD4s and K5Gs, etc, and I could not explain to myself how the designations matched a particular model, so imagine my glee when inspecting BH&D 6385 at Conway Street workshops to discover that it had 'Bristol' written on the engine block, whereas the bus beside it had 'Gardner'. On asking a mechanic I was told the Bristol was an AVW, and the Gardner a 5LW. My 10-year old brain could not cope with the normal syllabus of a preparatory school, but it took but seconds to work out what K5G, K6A and K6B meant, and about 10 minutes longer to differentiate the respective engine notes. As the BH&D buses always worked the same duties, and there were only seven K6Bs in the fleet at this time, I was soon taking money off my brother by repeatedly betting him that on shutting my eyes, I could give him the registration number of an approaching bus. I made *The Sting* look like nothing!

In the early postwar years, Brighton Hove & District boasted more AECs than Bristols, a legacy from the previous Tilling set up. This 1932 AEC Regent, seen here in 1953, sports a 1944 ECW body.

Southdown routes past our house were 14 to Haywards Heath, 17, to Horsham, 23, Crawley, 24 circular via Ditchling and Lewes, 30, Chelwood Gate, 32, Uckfield and 36, East Grinstead. The 14/17/23/24 were worked with an assortment of prewar TD4 and TD5 Leyland Titans (reminding me of LT STDs), mostly with lowbridge bodies by Beadle or Short, although none of the routes concerned went under low bridges! Route 17 proudly sported one of the 12 new Guy Arab IIIs with nicely-proportioned Northern Counties bodies, whilst the other three routes were single-deck operated, with Harrington rear-entrance bodies on Leyland Tiger TS6 chassis. None of these, except the NCME/Guys, made the charts, although the handsome Leyland Tiger PS1s with ECW bodies that worked the London-Brighton express service were great favourites, dropping a couple of points in the charts when Southdown replaced their sliding vents with half-drop windows.

We lived on Preston Road for four years, and if I wanted a change from travelling by BH&D bus, I used to catch a Corporation 46 or 46A trolleybus to Preston Drove, and walk down from there. Brighton Corporation buses were magnificent inside, and always reminded me of Odeon cinemas — Alhambrinal mosaic ceilings, polished woodwork and ribbed rubber covering on the bulkheads. The Weymann bodies on Brighton 1-44 were always top of

my trolleybus charts, closely followed by London Transport 1765-1891, but another item which endeared Brighton Corporation to me was the smartness of the crews, with their navy blue trousers and matching jackets with epaulettes, polished silver buttons with the Brighton coat-of-arms thereon, and black tie, worn with a white shirt with stiff collar. They were the cream . . .

During our sojourn on Preston Road, Brighton Corporation came off 35A and BH&D replaced most of its prewar stock with new K5Gs and K6Bs, taking delivery of 40 such buses in this period. During 1948-50, buses in the series 6394-6418 were delivered, many of them going on to routes running in the vicinity of my Hove school, replacing 1936 Dennis double-deckers on the 6 route, and I was most perplexed by the fact that there was a gap in the numbers between 6399 and 6407, and registrations EAP 8-11 and EPM 1-3 were missing. Where were they? A trip to London with my family provided the answer, when on leaving the Brighton train at Victoria station (day return in those days was 14/- [70p]!) I spotted a stranger in the forecourt; no London bus was he. No, it was BH&D 6404, on hire to London Transport together with six other BH&D K5Gs, where they worked routes 73 and 76 from Tottenham garage. These buses eventually came to Brighton in June 1950, still carrying London advertisements, and their stock numbers in super

London Transport Johnson sans serif type.

In 1951 we moved from London Road to Dyke Road. Here we had Corporation AECs on the 51 and 52s, handsome all-Leyland PD2s on Southdown's 12 route, and Tigers on the 27, with open-top Guy utilities on the seasonal service to the Devils Dyke. Our nearest BH&D route was the Hangleton to Lewes Road 14 route, worked solely by K6Bs 6386-90.

On the move again in 1953, back to BH&D-land, at Brunswick Square, between the Hove Sea Front and the Western Road shopping area. Except for some open-toppers, BH&D had by now replaced all of its prewar buses, plus the two utility Mk I Guy Arabs 6364/5, and they now had a relatively large fleet of 8ft wide buses, of the KS5G, KSW6G and KSW6B varieties. Southdown ran along the sea front, on routes 9, 10, 21 and 31. The first two routes were worked by Leyland PD1s either the 1946 ones with Park Royal bodies, or the 1947 batch with Leyland bodies. East Lancs-bodied Royal Tigers, of both front- and centre-entrance type, were on 21, and PD2/12 Titans handled the quarter-hour frequency 31, from Brighton to Portsmouth. These 8ft wide Titans had Leyland bodies, from 701-754 in three batches (the first 25 had open platforms and were later converted to enclosed platforms, as were all double-deck deliveries after 725); 755 to 764 were fitted with handsome Northern Counties bodies. Also using Hove sea front was the South Coast Express, running between Dover and Bournemouth and jointly worked by East Kent, Royal Blue and Southdown. In those days East Kent mainly used their FFN-registered Park Royal-bodied Royal Tigers, backed up by the 1947 PS1s which also had Park Royal-bodies; Royal Blue used either Bristol LL6B/Beadle or Bristol LS6B/ECW coaches, both types fitted with the familiar luggage rack on the roof, whilst Southdown provided LUF or LCD-registered Duple-bodied Royal Tigers (which I loathed), or PS1 Tigers, with assorted Beadle, Duple Harrington or Windover bodies.

In 1956 I went to work, and like my father before me I entered the film industry, as a camera assistant at Pinewood Studios. My return to the London Transport area was conspicuous by the lack of London bus variety. The RT was all-conquering, although the Pinewood routes were worked by Windsor, which had many top box RTs, and until mid-1956 we had a number of Craven RTs at WR, for variety. I was living in a flat at Wembley then, with only the 662 trolleybus route to relieve the RT-family monotony, although top-boxes were always welcome.

In 1960 I moved back to Sussex, albeit to Crawley where the Development Corporation was offering new flats at very low rents to entice people to the New Town, and it was too good an offer to miss. London Transport's Crawley garage had RTs (including one top box, RT 1034), RFs of both bus and coach (for the 710 Green Line) versions, a couple of Guy GS 26-seaters, and the last T-class bus in LTE service, a 15T13 AEC Regal III with Mann Egerton body. Southdown had a coach station at Crawley, which was a refreshment stop for the London-South Coast services, and beside this they built a small garage. Both have long since gone in the interests of road widening, rationalisation and shorter journey times, but Southdown's Crawley garage had a number of Guy Arab IVs in the early 1960s, these Park Royal-bodied buses working the 76/79 Crawley locals, 23 to Brighton and 23a to Handcross, whilst Haywards Heath worked 82, usually with the 1948 PD2s. I lived in Crawley until 1966, by which time Southdown was using NCME-bodied PD3 double-deckers in the town, and the Beadle chassisless coaches on the London service were being ousted by Leyland Leopards with Plaxton bodies, whilst Daimler Fleetlines had appeared in the town, LTE XF buses running in from East Grinstead on the 438.

Back to London, and Hampstead. RFs on 210 and MBs on the newly-introduced 268 local. The MBs have always reminded me of dinosaurs, and are so old-fashioned looking that they could well be a prehistoric design. In 1968 I bought a house in Barnes, giving me a good cross-section of London standard types — RMs (9, 33, 73), RMCs (715, 716, 716A), RFs (714), RMLs (37) and RTs (72).

In 1970 I worked on a film called *Lawman*. This was a Western, shot in Durango, Mexico, where I lived for six months. Greyhound-type bus operation appeared to be the mainstay of Mexican interurban operation, with three main companies working through Durango, on very long routes to places such as Mexico City, Mazatlan, El Paso and Mexicali. There was a town service, worked by three beaten-up US Dodge lorry chassis, on which were mounted locally-built dual-door bodies.

In 1973 I worked on *The Terminal Man*, a film made at Warner Bros. Burbank Studios, and so I lived in Hollywood for nine months. Buses didn't actually run past my door, but Southern California Rapid Transit District (RTD for short) line 89 ran close by, between Hollywoodland and Fairfax, being operated by standard GMC 5303 buses in a yellow, black and unpainted aluminium livery. A little further away, on Hollywood Boulevard, one encountered other RTD types, such as Flexibles and GMCs of the 1946-58 period. Other local operators within the Los Angeles area are the municipalities of Santa Monica and Long Beach, and the latter also operated a fleet of ex-LTE RLH, RT and RTL buses, on services to RMS *Queen Mary*, which is permanently moored at Long Beach. I

A standard GMC bus heads along Ventura Boulevard, Sherman Oaks, heading for downtown Hollywood. The Southern California Rapid Transit District has a large fleet of these buses in various lengths. Note the water-filled rubber bumper.

must say, having spent quite a long time in Southern California, I am always fascinated by the constant references to the lack of public transport facilities, insomuch as the greater Los Angeles area is well served by buses, in Downtown LA there is a well patronised minibus (actually midibus) route that is a circular service to the business district, there are peak hour express services from Downtown to the outer suburbs, known as *Freeway Flyers* and on the San Bernadino Freeway there is a bus-only reservation in the centre of the roadway allowing buses to travel at their own maximum speed, separated from other traffic. There is heavy TV and press advertising to inform the public of service alterations and innovations, and when I was last in LA, in November 1975, there was talk of experimental double-decker operation, possibly using Büssing buses.

I met my wife in Los Angeles. She is a lovely Irish colleen. And she took me home to Co. Wicklow. Well, all of the top box buses had gone from London, so there seemed little point in returning there, and I am not going to say much about the Irish bus scene, because I really said it all in *Buses Annual 1977*, except that all of the CIE PD2s have now gone, and the PD3s are on the way out. However, if you are a film technician, there are not too many work opportunities in Ireland. So we have moved — to Walton-on-Thames. Ever had the feeling you've been somewhere before? The Ts, STs and STLs have gone, and though we've *still* got RFs on the 218, after 24 years, their future seems uncertain. They are sights for sore eyes, as are the RTs at nearby Kingston. When it was the ubiquitous London bus, one did not really take

too much notice of the RT, but now, I marvel at those buses.

The RT design is, as I write, some 40-years old, and a number of the RTs still in service date from 1947 — a remarkable testament to the designers of Chiswick and Southall — and although only a handful of routes are now RT-operated, the buses look good for a number of years yet. But if you are of my age group, a ride on an RT is like a kaleidoscope of your own life. I was five when I rode on my first RT, albeit the 1939 version, and nine when I rode my first postwar RT. The interiors have not changed in 40 years, with their green and cream rexine around the windows, brown rexine below, the interior beading picked-out in red, and the solidness of the body. I spent most of the summer of 1977 riding on as many as I could, and I was amazed at the lack of body movement and the fact that windows and stanchions did not rattle. They really are, or probably by the time that you read this, have been, an integral part of my life thus far, and I will be very, very sorry to see them go.

Almost as sorry as when the top box STLs disappeared!

● *Since this article was written, a number of changes has taken place to the routes in the Shepperton area. The 237 has been withdrawn between Sunbury Village and Chertsey, this portion being covered by new London Country route 459, running from Addlestone Garage to Feltham, whilst east of Hounslow 237 has been extended over the 117 route to Shepherds Bush, working between that point and Sunbury with crew-operated Routemaster double-deckers, 117 having had its Routemasters replaced by OMO saloons.*

Door-to-Door service. *This was Brighton Corporation's last AEC in service, a 1950 Regent III with Weymann body, seen in 1967 in the erstwhile red and cream livery.*

Scarborough Seaside Special. *One of United's 'flying PUFs', a Bristol VRT/ECW diverted from Southdown to United, nears the Spa terminus at Scarborough, with the South Sands in the foreground and the Castle ruins in the background.*

Missing Municipalities. *A reminder of the Leeds City Transport fleet in the shape of the preserved 1940 AEC Regent with 56-seat Roe body, seen at Harrogate on the 1976 Trans-Pennine Run.*

The European Bus: Myth or Reality? *A standard Dutch city bus, a Hainje-bodied Daf SB200 on service in suburban Amsterdam.*

A cat may look at a king, and also, it seems, at something in the vicinity of a bus trailer belonging to one of the German private railway companies, at Kandern in the Black Forest (above) or, indeed, at a Greenslades coach (right).

Missing Municipalities

In just ten years 43 municipal bus fleets have disappeared from the scene. STEWART J. BROWN investigates the reasons, and recalls now-defunct undertakings.

In 1979 there are 49 local authority transport undertakings in the British Isles; at the start of 1969 there were 92. Of the 43 which have vanished in the past ten years some are already little more than a memory marked by a few non-standard types in a standardised fleet and soon to be forgotten completely; or perhaps remembered only by a preserved bus in a once-familiar livery.

Others will be remembered for pioneering work in one field or another. Wallasey operated the first Atlanteans; Manchester specified distinctive body styles; Glasgow foreshadowed future developments with its 34ft 6in long single-deck trolleybuses in 1958; Doncaster created a modern corporate image in 1972.

Or others will be remembered for their eccentricities. Walsall bought many strange vehicles; Morecambe & Heysham operated the last petrol-engined double-deckers in Britain in 1959 (and at 3.8mpg); the Stalybridge, Hyde, Mossley & Dukinfield Transport & Electricity Board owned the only Atkinson double-decker built — and had the longest name, usually abbreviated to SHMD.

The 1968 Transport Act, which created passenger transport executives in Merseyside, Tyneside, South East Lancashire and North East Cheshire, and West Midlands, caused the disappearance of 18 municipal transport departments in 1969. Originally each PTE was controlled by a passenger transport authority. In 1974 the reorganisation of local government brought control of the PTEs into the hands of the newly-formed metropolitan county councils.

To give some idea of the relative importance of each municipality the figures in brackets show their *approximate* fleet strengths when they were taken over.

The first PTE to get under way was West Midlands which on 1 October 1969 took over the municipal fleets of Birmingham (1,400), Walsall (268), West Bromwich (120), and Wolverhampton (288). Wolverhampton's green buses were mainly Guy Arabs with forward-entrance bodies. Wolverhampton had been an early convert to this concept in 1958 but remained loyal to front-engined chassis for double-deckers. The other three fleets were painted in different blue liveries and were latterly Daimler Fleetline purchasers — a model which featured prominently in the PTE's subsequent buying policy. The PTE adopted what was basically Birmingham's livery — smart or sombre depending on your viewpoint — and purchased Fleetlines with bodies to a Birmingham-style specification. Prior to its absorption by the PTE Birmingham had Britain's biggest municipal bus fleet.

Left: *Attractive Neepsend bodywork is fitted to this 1965 Leyland Atlantean of Sheffield.*

Below: *Ashton abandoned trolleybus operation in 1966, three years before the formation of Selnec. This all-Crossley trolleybus is seen in 1963, its final year.*

Walsall still operated trolleybuses in 1969 and West Midlands became the only trolleybus-operating PTE, retaining the system until 3 October 1970. Walsall in the 1960s had experimented with — and built up a large fleet of — short Daimler Fleetlines. At the other extreme it had Britain's biggest municipal double-decker, a 36ft long Daimler CRC6/36 with Cummins V6 engine at the rear offside corner, two staircases, two doors, 86 seats, and closed circuit television which allowed the driver to see the rear platform on a screen behind his cab!

The second PTE was Selnec — a catchy acronym for South East Lancashire North East Cheshire — which started operation on 1 November 1969. While it is quite possible that the good citizens of Birmingham are still unaware of the demise of Birmingham City Transport, their counterparts in Manchester can be in no doubt about the disappearance of their municipal buses.

Selnec took over no fewer than eleven municipal undertakings from Manchester (1,250) to Ramsbottom Urban Distict Council with its 12 vehicles. (Ramsbottom's final claims to fame, incidentally, were that it purchased the last old-style Leyland Titan — it entered service with Selnec in November 1969 — and that it was the last English

UDC to operate buses.) Between the extremes of Manchester and Ramsbottom were Ashton-under-Lyne (60), Bolton (249), Bury (96), Leigh (57), Oldham (180), Rochdale (130), Salford (271), SHMD (91), and Stockport (148). Each of these undertakings had its own vehicle policy and Selnec found itself the proud owner of AEC, Albion, Atkinson, Bedford, Bristol, Daimler, Dennis, Guy and Leyland buses with 19 different makes — and countless styles — of bodywork.

Ashton, Bury, Salford and Stockport were comparatively late buyers of Titans. Stockport's final deliveries included exposed-radiator open-platform rear-entrance Titans purchased in 1969! The others did at least run Fleetlines or Atlanteans too. Bolton had pioneered modern-looking bodywork for rear-engined chassis in 1963 and when the Bolton manager moved to Manchester in 1965 he had further developed his ideas there, culminating in the appearance of the striking Mancunian style of body with its large windows. Selnec further developed this body, eventually producing their own standard design against which all other double-deck bodies tend to be judged.

Leigh's double-deck fleet was entirely lowbridge or lowheight and the last ex-Leigh lowbridge Leyland

Left: *This Guy Arab of Birkenhead Corporation, photographed in 1963, was withdrawn before the undertaking passed to the Merseyside PTE. It had Massey bodywork.*

Right: *This Luton Corporation Bristol RE looks much the same as vehicles supplied by Bristol and ECW to nationalised companies.*

survived with Selnec's successor, Greater Manchester, until July 1977. The SHMD fleet included Walsall-style short Fleetlines.

Selnec selected a livery which was a complete break from those of its constituents who, between them, used most of the primary colours. Ashton and Leigh were blue; Bolton and Ramsbottom were maroon; Oldham was pommard; Bury, Salford and SHMD used green; Manchester and Stockport were red; Rochdale was mainly cream with blue relief — and, needless to say, no two used the same shade of colour. Selnec adopted a bold orange and white livery, a move which typified its bold approach to bus operation.

One other PTE took over its municipal constituents in 1969 and this was Merseyside, on 1 December. This saw the end of the last of the really big English municipal bus fleets with the acquisition by the PTE of Liverpool's 1,100 buses. Merseyside also incorporated two fleets on the south of the Mersey river — Birkenhead (225) and neighbouring Wallasey (75). Liverpool's standard bus was the Atlantean which could be described as the standard for Wallasey too, although no new buses — other than a 19-seat Bedford — had been purchased by that undertaking for seven years! However, on 10 December 1958 Wallasey had been the first Leyland Atlantean owner-

operator (beating Glasgow by five days). Birkenhead ran Atlanteans too, but had been buying exposed-radiator rear platform Titans as recently as 1967.

Merseyside compromised on liveries. North of the river Liverpool's green was retained while on the south, the PTE's Wirral division, the blue and cream livery reflected Birkenhead's colours and Wallasey's layout with a large expanse of cream.

The fourth PTE, Tyneside, got under way on 1 January 1970 when it took over the Newcastle-upon-Tyne and South Shields fleets. Newcastle had 352 buses, mainly Leylands, while South Shields, with 87 buses, had latterly favoured Daimlers. The PTE used Newcastle's yellow livery: South Shields' blue faded into oblivion. Newcastle's vehicle policy was continued with the purchase of Alexander-bodied Atlanteans by the PTE.

During 1970 the National Bus Company took over two municipal bus fleets. On 4 January United Counties acquired Luton. Luton's 70-strong fleet included ECW-bodied Bristol REs, a combination which suited its new owners well. Its double-deckers were mainly of Leyland group manufacture — lowbridge Titans and lowheight Lowlanders.

On 1 April the Exeter undertaking was sold to Devon General. Whereas Luton's dark red livery quickly gave way to United Counties green, Exeter's 65 green and cream Leylands (and exposed-radiator Guy Arab IVs) retained their livery for some 12 months before a decision was made to repaint them in Devon General red. The Exeter undertaking reportedly cost NBC £190,000.

A quiet period followed and in 1971 only one disappearance took place. This was the amalgamation of the Todmorden Joint Omnibus Committee fleet with that of the neighbouring (and larger) Halifax JOC. The resulting organisation was known as Calderdale JOC. Todmorden was a Leyland operator and 27 vehicles of this make, mostly short Leopards but including eight 20-year old Titan PD2s, passed to the Calderdale fleet on 6 September. The Halifax orange, green and cream livery replaced Todmorden's dark green and cream.

On 1 April 1973 Sunderland's 175 buses were added to the Tyneside PTE fleet one year earlier than they would have been under local government reorganisation when the PTE was to cover Tyne & Wear. Sunderland had achieved considerable fame during the 1960s when it had adopted one-man operation on a large scale, coupled to a zonal fare system. For its omo programme Sunderland had purchased rear-engined AEC, Bristol, Daimler and Leyland chassis, all with similarly-styled two-door bodywork (by Strachan or MCW) with sloping pillars. Sunderland's livery was green and off-white.

On 2 April 1973 Northern Ireland lost its sole municipal transport system when Belfast Corporation was acquired by the Northern Ireland Transport Holding Company. Initially it had been proposed that the Belfast fleet be merged with the existing Ulsterbus operation but instead a new company, Citybus Ltd, was formed to take over the 374-strong fleet. Belfast's red and ivory livery was retained but instead of buying Daimlers, Citybus ordered Leylands and Bristols.

On 1 June 1973 the largest surviving British municipal bus fleet, Glasgow, which had 1,318 buses, was handed over to the Greater Glasgow PTE. Glasgow's buses were mainly Leylands, including almost 700 Atlanteans. The PTE retained Glasgow's traditional green and yellow colours but used brighter shades; white relief instead of cream; and a more attractive style of application.

When 1974 dawned there were 66 municipal transport undertakings in Britain; when it closed there were only 51. Local government reorganisation on 1 April had taken its toll of 15.

The creation of metropolitan counties involved a redrawing of boundaries which brought some additional territory to the existing PTEs as well as creating two new ones.

West Midlands acquired Coventry's 308 buses, mostly Daimlers manufactured in that town. Coventry had revised its livery layout in 1973 into a West Midlands style, although retaining red rather than blue. From January 1974 West Midlands' blue/cream livery was adopted.

Merseyside expanded northwards to include Southport (69) and St Helens (127). The former operated a mainly Leyland fleet, including Leyland Nationals, while the latter favoured AEC Swifts. St Helens never operated rear-engined double-deckers (its newest were Titans) and Southport had only one batch of newly-delivered Atlanteans. Both fleets were red and cream. Merseyside in October 1974 revised its livery, choosing a light green and cream for the whole fleet to replace the previous Liverpool green and Wirral blue liveries, as well as the newly-acquired red liveries.

Selnec became Greater Manchester and at the same time acquired 130 maroon and white buses from Wigan corporation. Wigan was a Leyland user — mainly Titans but with a number of Atlanteans and Panthers. Like many other Lancashire municipalities it was a late purchaser of Titans, buying them until 1968. Wigan had favoured forward entrances for its buses since 1959.

West Yorkshire was the bigger of the two new PTEs. It took over Bradford (325), Halifax and Calderdale (225), Huddersfield (219) and Leeds (700). Originally the PTE proposed that its district structure be indentified by distinctive liveries based on buttermilk relieved by blue for Bradford, orange for Calderdale (incorporating Halifax), red for Kirklees (Huddersfield), and green for Leeds. Before 1 April a few buses from each fleet were repainted in these schemes while some in Halifax received dark green and cream liveries in various styles. However, in the end a standard livery of verona green and buttermilk replaced the four municipal liveries, although the distinctive district names survived until early 1977 when the fleet name MetroBus was introduced.

Halifax and Huddersfield were Fleetline buyers; Bradford and Leeds bought both Fleetlines and Atlanteans and this policy was continued by the PTE.

The new South Yorkshire PTE combined Doncaster (120), Rotherham (130) and Sheffield (660). Doncaster, a Daimler operator, had a modern image created for it by a local art college. This retained the fleet's traditional red but with a lilac and white relief band, and used modern lettering for fleet numbers and the Doncaster Transport fleetname. This was without equal in recent municipal bus history and its obliteration by the PTE was a sad loss. Rotherham, too, ran Fleetlines, while Sheffield's fleet included Bristol VRTs, Daimler Fleetlines, and Leyland Atlanteans with a variety of bodywork. Both Rotherham and Sheffield had blue liveries; the former

The enlarged Lancaster undertaking adopted a blue and white livery. A 1958 East Lancs bodied Leyland PD3 acquired from Burnley & Pendle passes a 1977 Leyland Leopard/Alexander outside Morecambe depot.

blue and ivory, the latter cream relieved by three blue bands. The PTE adopted an insipid livery of coffee and cream . . . or cold tea and milk?

In passing, it is worth noting that the Huddersfield and Sheffield fleets had, until shortly before the formation of the Yorkshire PTEs, been involved in joint ownership agreements with the National Bus Company and before that with successive railway companies.

Also on 1 April 1974 two existing Lancashire municipal undertakings were enlarged by being amalgamated with their neighbours while in South Wales a new authority, Rhymney Valley District Council, combined three existing Urban District Council fleets.

The larger of the new Lancashire fleets was Blackburn which now included the Darwen undertaking. Before April Blackburn had 102 buses in an attractive bright green and cream livery while Darwen had 33 in traditional red and cream. Darwen's newest double-deckers were 1969 Titans; since then it had purchased only Bristol REs. Blackburn was a Leyland user, favouring Atlanteans with home-town built East Lancs bodies. The combined authority chose a combined livery of dark red, dark green and white, sadly using less attractive shades of colours

than had its constituents.

Lancaster was the smaller of the new fleets and now incorporated Morecambe & Heysham. The old Lancaster undertaking had 36 buses and Morecambe had 48. Lancaster favoured Leylands; Morecambe's newest buses were AEC Swifts and Seddons. A new blue and white livery replaced Lancaster's red and Morecambe's green and the new Lancaster undertaking standardised on Alexander-bodied Leyland Leopards. It had the distinction of being the last municipal operator of a half-cab single-decker — a 1952 Daimler CVG5 which in 1977 provided a special service to commemorate the Queen's Silver Jubilee.

Bedwas & Machen, Caerphilly, and Gelligaer were the fleets which combined to form Rhymney Valley. The Bedwas & Machen fleet of eight buses included four modern Leyland Leopards and also the last side-gangway lowbridge bus to be built in Britain; this was a 1968 Massey-bodied Leyland Titan PD3 with traditional exposed radiator and rear entrance with platform doors.

Bedwas had another claim to fame: a quaint notice (to be read with a Welsh accent) adorned all its buses worded (in 1974!) 'NOTICE The Travelling Public are herewith respectfully informed that the consumption

99

Only one of Gelligaer's Northern Counties-bodied Bristol VRTs received the final livery in which pale green replaced dark green.

of fish & chips is strictly forbidden on the Council's Omnibuses'. Savour the wording ... The Travelling Public ... consumption ... Omnibuses ... all with a flavour of bygone days. 'Contravention of this order initiates contravention of the Undertaking's conditions of acceptance of travel', it continued sternly, leading to a final warning: 'This notice must not be defaced'! What a fuss over a fish supper. The populace of Bedwas were fortunate if that was the most serious anti-social behaviour they had to contend with.

Caerphilly, too, was a Leyland user — Leopards, Titans, and three new Atlanteans in a 31-strong fleet. However Gelligaer — also 31 strong — was different. It had AEC Reliances and Swifts and its most recent purchases had been Bristols, an unusual choice for a small UDC fleet. The latter were ECW-bodied REs and Northern Counties-bodied VRTs.

The new Rhymney Valley District Council faced a mini-Selnec problem. It acquired AEC, Bedford, BMC, Bristol and Leyland buses and its constituents' liveries were dark blue and cream (Bedwas & Machen); dark green and cream (Caerphilly) and an attractive red, white and pale green — or dark green

— for Gelligaer. The new authority chose brown, yellow and ivory as its livery, an unusual but not unattractive combination.

On 1 October 1976 Douglas (Isle of Man) lost its primrose and red municipal bus fleet to the newly-formed Isle of Man National Transport which also took over IoM Road Services. Douglas had 41 buses including AEC Regents and Leyland Leopards. The horse tramcar fleet remained in municipal ownership.

The last fleet to go was Waveney. Waveney's wavering ceased on 3 December 1977 after a long period of uncertainty. It, and its predecessor, Lowestoft, had long been involved in discussions with Eastern Counties and various co-ordination agreements (or disagreements?) had been discussed over the years. At the end it was operating ten two-door ECW-bodied AEC Swifts and a few double-deckers. Its route passed to Eastern Counties, but its dark maroon and cream buses did not.

Which leaves 49 local authority transport undertakings, many of which received new names in 1974 and 1975 when local government was reorganised. But that, as they say, is another story ...

HUMBERSIDE BEFORE THE BRIDGE

DAVID KAYE

A Connor & Graham Leyland Atlantean, ex-Ribble, outside C&G's Easington garage.

On 1 April 1974 a new county appeared on the maps of England — Humberside covering 1,356sq miles and comprising much of the former East Riding of Yorkshire, the Goole area of the old West Riding and the most northerly 600sq miles of Lincolnshire. The southern boundary was a jagged compromise, owing to the pressure brought by the Yarborough family to have their Brocklesby Park estates left in Lincolnshire.

The unifying factor was to be the Humber Bridge, with its world record central span for a suspension bridge of 4,626ft and twin towers reaching a height of 518ft above the mean level of the river beneath. Forty years ago preliminary plans had been drawn up to build such a bridge at a cost of £2.5m. The Second World War delayed any practical measures until 1959, when the Humber Bridge Act was passed setting up the Humber Bridge Board. Work began in 1972 with the projected cost for the structure now having risen to £27m. Although the North Tower was completed by the following

year, unstable geological strata on the southern shore meant that the other tower did not reach its full height until late in 1976. By that time the estimated cost of the project had reached nearly £60m. Meanwhile Britain's last regular paddle steamer service, using the *Lincoln Castle* continued between New Holland and Corporation Pier, Hull.

Humberside contains a score of towns varying in size from the city of Kingston-upon-Hull (276,000) and the fishing port of Grimsby (100,000) through the medium-sized seaside resorts of Cleethorpes (37,500) and Bridlington (27,500), down to small country towns like Brigg (5,000) and Market Weighton (3,400). It contains only one truly industrial town, the steel centre of Scunthorpe (68,100), the inland port of Goole (17,800) and the growing tourist, coal and petro-chemical port of Immingham (11,500). The county town, inherited from the East Riding, is Beverley (16,900), with its famous Minster.

In North Humberside the principal

operators are Kingston-upon-Hull City Transport (previously featured in *Buses Annual 1976*) and East Yorkshire Motor Services Ltd, a former BET member, which passed to the NBC in 1969. In South Humberside the two equivalents are Grimsby & Cleethorpes Transport Joint Committee and the Lincolnshire Road Car Company Ltd, which has been nationalised since the setting up of the BTC in the late 1940s. There are other similarities between the two halves as well. Whereas East Yorkshire runs the town services of Bridlington, Lincolnshire has a similar function in Scunthorpe. Turning to the role of independents we find other cases of symmetry. Boddy's Motors (Bridlington) Ltd, with their 22 coaches are mirrored by Granville Tours Ltd of Grimsby with a fleet of 20. There are few independent operators of any size in the county, and I suppose that you could say that Connor & Graham of Easington on the north bank of the great river are the counterparts of the famous Daisy Bus Service of Broughton,

101

near Brigg in the south of the county.

However, let us first look at the unique case as far as Humberside is concerned — an independent operating all a town's local routes. In Beverley the internal transport is provided by Cherry Coaches, which takes its name from proprietor Mr R. P. Cherry and not from the livery, which is, in fact, black and cream. Mr Cherry began his service in 1932, and there were in 1977 three routes operating, one of which appropriately goes via the Cherry Tree Estate! To work these there are three single-deck buses available, a Ford R192/Willowbrook B45F, a Ford R1014/Willowbrook B45F and what is probably the only Seddon Pennine IV in the county, which also seats 45 passengers. In recent years Cherry Coaches has built up a network of works services to the Hawker-Siddeley factory at Brough; these are from Beverley & Wallington (1961), from Beverley & Cottingham (1969) and from Howden (1970). For this there is a fleet of Ford 192s, R1014s and R1114s, plus an ex-City of Oxford AEC Renown.

The mention of Beverley conjures up in the mind the Beverley Bar buses of East Yorkshire with their specially-designed domed roofs to enable them to pass under the last remaining gateway of the town. This structure was built of 125,000 bricks in 1409/10 at a cost of just under £98! Within the last few years it has been by-passed by a new inner relief road, which serves the Sowgate bus station. Nevertheless, even in the Silver Jubilee summer of 1977 there were some Beverley Bar buses still to be found in the area. AEC Bridgemasters were to be found at that period on the town routes of Bridlington, which like most seaside towns has augmented local routes during the peak summer period. For example whereas during the winter routes 83, 83W, 183, 283 & 383 (all variations of Bridlington-Flamborough) run on roughly a two-hourly headway out to the famous lighthouse (with a journey in between terminating in the village itself), during the height of the holiday season it is increased to a half-hourly frequency for the entire

route, with shorter journeys in between going as far as Sewerby Park on the eastern periphery of Bridlington. Another difference in the summer is that the buses run along the sea front, whilst for the rest of the year they are diverted inland. During 1977 the town routes were operated by a variety of two-man AEC Bridgemasters and Renowns and one-man Leyland Leopards and Bristol Vrs.

Bridlington bus station sees some routes which are interworked with other NBC members. Routes 44, 44A, 45 & 45A (to York and Leeds) are run jointly with West Yorkshire, whilst routes 120, 121 & 122 (to Scarborough) are worked in conjunction with United.

To serve the holidaymakers, Boddy's Motors runs a comprehensive set of excursions, which are repeated each week during the season. These include a daily trip down the coast to the Hornsea Potteries (with their miniature replica of London General's B240), with other half-day visits to the local stately homes of Burton Agnes Hall and Sledmere House. Longer runs are to the Flamingo Park Zoo, Hull, Ravenscar, Scarborough and Whitby. There are also those fascinating 'oldies' the evening mystery drives. Boddy's (which remains a family business) began operating horse-drawn landaus in 1900 (still a feature of Bridlington's promenade scene). After many years with an ivory and red livery, in 1975 Boddy's changed over to one of Dover white and flame (a variety of orange). Although in the past AEC Reliances have formed the largest group in the fleet, recent purchases have been of Bedford YRTs and YMTs.

Easington had the honour of being the site of the first North Sea gas terminal in Britain. It is also the home of Connor & Graham Ltd, which was formed in 1921, and is still run by the Graham family. The main route begins just south of the depot at Kilnsea (at the base of the trunk-like Spurn Point), and takes passengers for 84 minutes through a string of villages and the little market town of Hedon into Hull. The mainstay of this service, which at

times requires three vehicles for its operation, is a pair of ex-Ribble Leyland Atlanteans, and a 48-seat Bedford VAM. The dark maroon and cream buses also work an additional single return trip between the terminii via Sunk Island, where 6,000 acres of the Humber marshes were reclaimed for agricultural use during the 18th century. Of the other vehicles in their 1977 fleet, all but three were second-hand, and were made up of no fewer than nine different types of chassis, four of which were Ford Transits. The newest was a Bedford YMT.

The port of Goole is a meeting point for a number of operators, but only Lincolnshire has a sub-depot in the town. Lincolnshire operates the local routes with Bristol LH and LHS buses to Swinefleet (159) and to Hook and Airmyn (164). Goole is linked with Scunthorpe by route 118, which wanders through most of the villages in North Axholme. National Bus is also represented in Goole by East Yorkshire and West Riding. The former runs an hourly service using Bristol VRs to Hull (route 5), whilst the latter use similar vehicles on route 140, also on an hourly headway, to Pontefract (with occasional journeys being extended to Castleford). The two services do actually have connections at North Street. Until a few years ago this gave a variety of liveries, with the shades of West Riding green complimenting the attractive dark blue and primrose of East Yorkshire, but now passengers just see a uniformity of National poppy red!

Twin independent operators work the half-hourly route out of Goole along the road to Doncaster — Reliance of Stainforth (alias R. Store Ltd) and Blue Line of Armthorpe (alias Samuel Morgan Ltd). The fleet of dark and mid-blue double-deckers and light blue and cream single-deckers terminate alternately at Christ Church, Doncaster and Emerson Avenue, Stainforth. Generally Roe-bodied Guy Arabs work the Goole-Doncaster route, with the occasional journey on Sundays one-man operated using Daimler Fleetlines or Fords. The Ford R1014s and R1114s work the Stainforth service, which is one-man

A Lincolnshire ex-Western SMT Bristol VRT with ECW body, at Scunthorpe bus station.

operated. The one-man services use TIM ticket machines, while the crew services use the Willebrew system.

Scunthorpe's bus station sees three rather different categories of routes being run by Lincolnshire. The first of these consists of the town services (routes 300 to 312), which were being worked in 1978 mainly by the remaining Bristol Lodekkas (FS, FL and FLF models). Each route has its own colour code, which is used on timetables and on bus stops. Weekday frequences vary from 10 minutes to 40 minutes, and in all 18 buses are needed to cover rush hour workings. This includes route 311 to the suburb of Ashby, which must be the only instance of joint routes being worked by an NBC member and *two* independents, all in different liveries. Hornsby Coaches, in two tones of blue, uses double-deckers; on the other hand the entire fleet of the third member of the triumvirate consists of a solitary yellow and cream Willowbrook-bodied Bedford single-decker, making Ubique rather unique!

The second class of route using

Scunthorpe bus station is the rural service (numbered between 101 and 179, with considerable gaps). These are the habitat for a mixed batch of ageing Bristol MW5Gs, LH buses and dual-purpose vehicles, Bristol VRs (both native and ex-Scottish) and Leyland Nationals. They link the town with Barton-upon-Humber, Brigg, Doncaster, Gainsborough, Grimsby, Goole and Lincoln. The last group of routes (320-326) are those which run to the outskirts of the steel town to such delightfully evocative destinations as Ore Preparation Plant, Appleby Extensions, Anchor Medium Site and Engineering Workshops. The earliest journey of the day is one on route 322 starting at 05.12 for the Lysaghts Works.

Unlike many other towns both Grimsby and its intertwined neighbour Cleethorpes were late into the field of municipal transport, relying on trams and buses run by the Great Grimsby Street Tramways Company Ltd (a member of the Provincial empire) until 1925 and 1929 respectively. Both places went

through a trolleybus period, Grimsby's starting in 1926 and Cleethorpes in 1937. The two undertakings were merged in January 1957, whilst their joint trolleybus fleet was withdrawn three years later. Grimsby-Cleethorpes operate three routes in conjunction with Lincolnshire. Route 45 to Immingham Docks is usually worked by the newer members of the growing municipal fleet of Daimler Fleetlines, whilst normally AEC Reliance and Swift single-deckers are employed on the ten minute headway route 16 out to the large Willows Estate on the western outskirts of the conurbation. The third route, 4X, runs only on Saturdays to Laceby (Charles Avenue) supplementing Lincolnshire routes 114, 135 and 136, and is again single-decker worked. Incidentally the suffix 'X' does not indicate an express route, as in the case of the majority of operators, but instead was introduced by a previous general manager to denote either a variation of route (instead of the more normal 'A' suffix) or else

103

because Lincolnshire already had a route of that number (eg 4: Lincoln-Brigg). Three unusual batches of vehicles are to be found in the Grimsby-Cleethorpes fleet. There are the ex-Nottingham City Swifts with their tall, heavy-looking Northern Counties bodywork which followed an earlier purchase of AEC Regents from that source. Secondly, there is a quartet of Fleetline single-deckers with Willowbrook bodywork with dual entrance/exit, like all single-deckers in the undertaking. Finally, there is the one and only open-top Bridgemaster, which appears on the Cleethorpes promenade route during the height of the summer season.

The expanding Lincolnshire independent Applebys works into Grimsby from two of its depots, at Caistor and at North Somercotes, where in December 1976 the former Lincolnshire route 50C from Mablethorpe was taken over and amalgamated with the existing Saltfleet service, questioning the travelling public as to what times they would like to see the buses running. Normally Applebys uses a mixture of Bedford and Ford coaches, but sometimes an ex-Hudson Ford bus appears instead at their terminus on the forecourt of the Brighowgate bus station.

Some special business flights into the Humberside Airport at Kirmington (between Brigg and Grimsby) are met by the pair of Bedford VAS coaches operated by Peter Sheffield of Cleethorpes, whose fleet of 40 mauve and white vehicles includes no less than 20 Ford R1014s and R1114s. To help in the school contract work and industrial journeys out to Fisons' factory at Immingham and Laportes Industries at Stallingborough, Sheffield also has a pair of AEC Regent Vs as well as a couple of ex-City of Oxford Dennis Lolines.

The company address of *Norfolk House*, Welholme Road, Grimsby for Granville Tours Ltd is a clue that it is a subsidiary of Norfolk Motor Services of Great Yarmouth with whom it shares a common modernised blue livery and fleet numbering scheme. The 20 Ford coaches are mainly concerned with long distance tours and with local excursion traffic.

A purchaser of rare vehicles is Daisy Bus Services Ltd of Broughton, a village near Brigg. At one time Daisy ran the one and only Dennis Pelican, and at present amongst the small fleet of eight vehicles is a striking Bedford VAL70 with Caetano Estoril bodywork. In 1937 it bought out another small independent in the area, Ermine Coaches (Ermine Street runs close by), and in 1960 acquired Portman Coaches of Scunthorpe, and with that firm a share of the excursion traffic of that town. Their main stage carriage routes are from Broughton and Santon to the South Iron Works, although a market day route operates into Brigg on Thursdays, supplementing Lincolnshire's 171 journeys.

What of the future, when the great bridge is open? It is hoped to run joint services across it between such places as Scunthorpe and Hull, operated by East Yorkshire and Lincolnshire. In addition a transport interchange will be built adjacent to

Top: *A Ford R192 with Plaxton Derwent 45-seat body in the fleet of Cherry Coaches, Beverley.*
Above: *A 1962 Guy Arab IV with 73-seat Roe body in the Blue Line fleet of Samuel Morgan Ltd.*

Barton-upon-Humber railway station, and this will include a car park for the many people who may well prefer to park'n'ride than to pay a hefty toll charge, and then have the problem of finding a parking lot in Hull. It could become the longest and best patronised of any such service in Britain.

Shell-shocked. Two Scottish shell-bedecked buses, retained for purely decorative reasons. This bus (left), seen in 1953, has long been a familiar attraction at Leven, Fife. Its origins are unknown. The Burlingham Baby Seagull-bodied Bedford OWB (below left), was seen at Baile dhubh, on North Uist, in 1974.

Below: This 1964 Ford 676E with Duple body was new to Winkle, Willenhall. By 1977 it had become an essential part of Mary Connors and her Human Cannon Act. Presumably only girls of the proper calibre need apply...

East Anglian Contrasts

Photographs by G. R. MILLS

An AEC Regal IV with Park Royal body which did not stray far when it was sold by Ipswich Corporation. It is seen (below) in 1968 in Corporation service, and (foot of page) in 1974 with the Ipswich Coach Co.

AEX 82B, an AEC Reliance with short-length Pennine 39-seat body, was new to Great Yarmouth Corporation in 1964 (above), and is seen after sale to Lowestoft Corporation in 1970 (left).

Leicester Corporation 196, a 1964 AEC Reliance with Marshall 47-seat two door body, at Abbey Park Road in 1971.

The same bus after it had been bought in 1971 by Colchester Corporation, and converted by Willowbrook to become a 53-seat one-door bus.

The same bus again, after Colchester Corporation had sold it to Lewingtons, of Cranham, Essex, and seen in 1976.

This AEC Reliance with Plaxton Highway 55-seat body started life in 1963 with Irvine, Salsburgh. By 1970 it had passed to D. R. MacGregor's Hedingham & District fleet.

During 1970, 652 GVA was bought from Hedingham & District by Colchester Corporation, and it is shown here leaving Colchester bus station in 1974.

After working in Scotland and England, 652 GVA passed to Wales, and Bebb, Llantwit Fadre in 1975.

This ex-Ribble 1958 Burlingham-bodied
Leyland Titan PD3/4 was loaned by
Ensign, Hornchurch, to Southend
Corporation before sale to China Motor
Bus, Hong Kong, in 1975. KCK 920 is
seen (right) in 1974 ready for repainting.
In 1975 (below) it is seen in service with
Southend.

Interchange

London Transport STL type buses in Morden station yard in wartime days.

Co-ordination between different transport operators is nothing new. In London there is a long history of interesting schemes of this type, as CHARLES F. KLAPPER recalls.

In lectures to busmen I am very apt to use the electrical engineer's symbol for alternating current to indicate the yoyo-like fluctuations of fortune in the bus industry. Depression is followed by a wave of prosperity and then again by depression with monotonous regularity.

Thus George Shillibeer's innovation of the bus as a vehicle that could ply for hire the length of its route (carefully selected, for example, avoiding 'the stones', though they might be) led to a boom in bus traffic in 1829 and 1830, only to be followed by the usual results of competition, ie depression, which by 1832 had so impressed the majority of proprietors that they formed associations for the regulation of the bus business.

Successive peaks of prosperity may be associated with the Great Exhibition of 1851, the peak of Victorian prosperity in 1896, the introduction through the London General Omnibus Company of successful lightweight motor buses (the B-type) that were

economical to run and put the motor bus business on the road to prosperity; other manufacturers followed, notably Leyland and Straker-Squire, and after the 1914 war the development of the rural bus, stimulated by the number of ex-soldiers who had learned something about motor transport in the Army (my brother, on leave in 1915, talked learnedly about Lindley preselective gearboxes because his unit had been dished out with a Commer lorry) produced a flood of competitive bus and coach services that called for official regulation in the Road Traffic Act of 1930 and finally the 'Golden Age' of bus operation in 1951 when rationing effects and a cinema boom made traffic all day like the rush hour and prospective car-owners were quoted four years for delivery. At this period several quite sound bus operators started services to small hamlets which only a year or two later were sources of wonderment as to whom had taken leave of their senses!

The reverse flow in our alternating current diagram is represented by the troughs of bus traffic, occasioned in the period after 1870 by the competition of horse tramways; after 1907 by high motor bus repair costs and electric tramway competition coupled with police harassment; from 1922 through the 1920s ('the roaring twenties') severe competition shown in London by the wave of something like 500 independent buses; after 1939 petrol rationing returned as in the 1914-18 war but much more sensibly than in 1917 although some of the traffic commissioners were rather unreasonable and caused the withdrawal of sorely-needed coach services and harassed bus undertakings by requisitioning garage premises; the final drop in traffic is one that began in 1968 and seems unlikely to disappear since it is largely caused by the proliferation of the private car. When it became apparent that Beeching had left the railways in no fit state to maintain rural services and that bus companies were in like case the General Post Office began post bus services on 20 February 1967.

Now we may come to the conclusion that co-ordination was not entirely the work of Lord Ashfield, or Albert Stanley as he then was. It began 80 years earlier in 1831. By September of that year the bus idea had become so popular in London that the New Road service alone, from Paddington to the Bank, via Kings Cross, had 90 buses running on it. A meeting at the Wheatsheaf in Edgware Road, presided over by George Shillibeer himself, decided to withdraw 33 buses from the New Road services and to spread them out from 08.00 to 22.00 at 3 minute intervals. Regulation was effected by the appointment of inspectors who worked on behalf of the proprietors, or the owners of the 'times'. The times of bus services continued to be a saleable commodity until the final day of horse buses, when in 1906 the British Electric Traction Company purchased some and found that, owing to the operations of the Vanguard motor buses, they were of no value.

Inspection of tickets, when they were introduced, became another function shared by all the proprietors of 'the times' of a service. The residents of Poplar and Limehouse had hardly to voice their dissatisfaction with their bus services before a Blackwall Association was formed. The largest of the associations was the Atlas and Waterloo Association.

It therefore becomes apparent that joint payment of common functionaries, such as inspectors and timekeepers, dates back to the earliers days of the bus in London. The comfortable atmosphere of the horse bus owners was upset after 1905 by the setting up of the London Motor Omnibus Co Ltd. It started in the very month I was born, so that I grew up with the idea that bus rivalry was the accepted thing; Vanguard, as the LMOCo Ltd named its first buses, intending other names to be available for other services, respected no association rules and acted as a pirate to existing horse bus owners. Moreover, taking a cue from the twopenny tube (the Central London Railway) it became motor bus practice to charge about half the usual horse bus fare.

So the motor bus produced some interesting, although unintentional, results. The newly-electrified lines of underground railway (the Metropolitan and Metropolitan District systems) had not turned out very profitable; the new tube railways were not nearly as remunerative as had been confidently predicted; the London County Council had become disillusioned with the idea of building shallow subways across the central area to remedy the gaps in the tramway system; lastly, the motor bus had proved a vast source of unforeseen expenditure as a result of which many operators contemplated going through the bankruptcy courts.

The year 1907 was a dismal one for motor bus owners, who were harried by the police because of noise; the Salisbury-Jones group which included Vanguard reorganised on 4 April 1907 as the Vanguard Motor Bus Co Ltd. Many operators fell by the wayside, including the London Power Omnibus Co Ltd, with over 70 vehicles; the Associated Omnibus Co Ltd gave up its motors and reverted to horses; Birch Bros gave up its motors; early in 1908 the Star Omnibus Co Ltd joined the throng of dispirited proprietors.

First of all the Central London Railway was persuaded to increase its 2d fare to 3d and various motor bus companies then were able to increase their fares. The London Electrobus Co Ltd made a feature of advertising 'We maintain the old fares'. But the old fares did not produce enough revenue and the London Electrobus rolling-stock was soon translated to the quieter atmosphere of Brighton — no doubt at bargain secondhand prices.

Several happenings developed from the meetings of bus and underground magnates; the three principal bus operators — General, Vanguard and Union Jack — amalgamated as one strong undertaking, the London General Omnibus Co Ltd, as from 1 July 1908. It weeded out some of the vehicles likely to cause trouble with the police and a move was made to equip all the vehicles with destination and route boards to police specification. At the same time, service numbers which had been introduced by George Samuel Dicks, traffic manager of Vanguard on 30 April 1906, were applied throughout the General fleet, to horse services as well as the motor.

On 30 August 1909 Sir Edward Henry, Commissioner of Metropolitan Police, issued new regulations for motor buses. There were stringent limitations on weight and enemies of the motor bus (and they were many!) thought nobody would be able to continue in business after they came into force. Rather foolishly, A.L.C. Fell, the London County Council Tramways manager, who believed in the freight motor vehicle, allowed himself to be quoted as

Thomas Tilling's first motor buses were 34-seat Milnes-Daimlers which ran from Peckham to Oxford Circus in 1904.

saying 'That there would be no motor bus outside a museum in ten years' time'. The chief engineer of the London General Company perhaps looked upon this as a challenge; he had already had a success in sorting out the extraordinary variety of makes in the fleet so that they were segregated by makes in their respective garages, simplifying the stocking of spares and the fitting of parts. Now Frank Searle suggested to the LGOC board that use should be made of covered premises at Walthamstow for building their own buses. The first attempt as this was not altogether successful and only 61 of the resulting X-type were built. Snide reports called it a Daimler-Wolseley-Straker and Searle cheerfully admitted indebtedness to all the longer-lasting components of other chassis. So far from the motor bus being doomed, the new lightweight B-type bus which the General now produced was silent and very light on repairs and maintenance. Bus operation became profitable for perhaps the first time.

This led to a wave of other bus companies, some with B-type buses like Associated, and some with other chassis, like the Great Eastern of London, which had Straker-Squire vehicles or London Central with Leyland, but the interesting fact was that by December 1911, it was already apparent that the B-type, introduced only on 18 October 1910, was a winner and that the affairs of the General were going to see a remarkable turn for the better. This resulted in the Underground group initiating talks with the LGOC with a view to buying the bus company. It is calculated that altogether £227 was paid for each £100 share of the bus company. Immediate changes were made in the directors, some of the old horse lovers being retired; they had angered Frank Searle immensely by ignoring his new X-type bus (upon which and the B-type their whole future depended) to look at some horses just back from Army manoeuvres.

A new London General Omnibus Co Ltd, with an enlarged radius of operation, as defined in the articles of association, was registered on 25 July 1912. Just before that, on Bastille Day, 1912, 14 July, the exciting step was taken of running services beyond the old limits of a 15-mile radius from Charing Cross.

These services, extending far into the country around London, were at once a success. In the planning stage an hourly headway was proposed for the Windsor service with connection from Hounslow Barracks station. In the event, a 5-minute service was demanded on Sundays, and a 30-minute one on weekdays, with extras on Wednesdays and Saturdays. Other services, intended to be on Sundays and holidays only, were run every day of the week from the start; in this class were the route to Romford from Bow Road station, and that to St. Albans from Golders Green. Clinging to tradition, the service to Windsor at first started from a public house, the 'Bell', but it was then realised that it was neither being hauled by horses that wanted a drink nor provided by buses previous to the B-type that were thirsty for radiator water. By August alternate cars were announced as going to Hounslow Barracks station only and the number, that began as being 62 in July, had been changed to 81; a series of numbers were allocated to services that connected with underground facilities from 80 upwards. These ran via Putney Bridge, Richmond, Northfields, Ealing Broadway, Golders Green, Highgate (now Archway), Finsbury Park, Bow Road, and Barking. Through facilities were quite informal; no through tickets were issued.

On 13 June 1912 the Associated Equipment Co Ltd was registered; it was hived off as a separate company to facilitate the sale of B-type buses to other operators. In June of the following year, H. E. Blain, the tramways manager of West Ham, was induced to join the Underground group as purchasing officer, by October 1913, his merits as a traffic manipulator were recognised by his appointment as operating manager of the LGOC. When he was appointed to the West Ham general managership back in 1903 he had already given an example of his tart speech. He had deformed feet, and the chairman of the tramways committee asked him how as a cripple he would be able to manage the West Ham Tramways. The reply was that he proposed to manage the tramways with his head not his feet. As traffic manager (and 1913-21 general manager) of the General he soon made his influence apparent by inaugurating services across Wanstead Flats, to Woodford Bridge and every day through Epping Forest, to Buckhurst Hill at first and even under the stress of bus shortage in the war, during 1915, to Loughton. The Blain regime was also notable for a revival of central area services, such as Liverpool Street and Victoria (advertised for a month only in December 1913) and Victoria and Kings Cross stations by two routes which lasted only a few months, although possibly fostered by temporary competition. Also in 1913 Blain introduced all-night buses on routes from Cricklewood and Willesden to Liverpool Street. These were developed to their present scope soon after the London Traffic Act of 1924, but at first

included a number of trips such as 12.45 from Ludgate Circus to Turnham Green, afterwards expanded to eight trips from Liverpool Street via Walham Green to Turnham Green.

The period of independent buses (1922-33) left a permanent mark in the pattern of London services. There were a number of services such as 511 Chingford to Stratford, launched by the East London Association to replace a suspended municipal tram service (which was rapidly replaced). Groups, among whom Aro Omnibus Co Ltd was prominent, sometimes produced most ingenious routes to avoid restricted streets; one, in particular, which survives as 236 between Finsbury Park and Leytonstone across Hackney Marshes, dodged Dalston Junction in a masterly way.

Fortune favours the brave and the City Motor Omnibus Co Ltd was nothing if not bold; inspired by the 1924 Road Traffic Act it began a distinctive service of its own right across central London on 7 December 1924 at first as 517, from Highgate to Peckham Rye via Victoria. On 21 January 1925 the service, renumbered 536, was diverted to Brockley Rise and on 14 April 1927 it was extended to Beckenham. Eventually United, and Archway (Birch Bros) as well as City buses, all in their distinctive livery of spanish tan and brown were operating the service, which was extended to West Wickham on Sundays. Other services, run by associations of independent proprietors, were devised to avoid restricted streets and provide long through routes; there were a number, but the most famous were 525, Enfield Town and Cubitt Town and 526, North Finchley and Wandsworth Bridge in which Birch Brothers took a large part. A number of short services were added to the network by the independents, such as Stroud Green and Forty Hill; the length of Liverpool Road, which had been deserted by the LCC in horse-tram days without electrification; and Trundleys Road, New Cross, which required single-deckers owing to a low bridge.

After the formation of the London Passenger Transport Board, T. E. Thomas (afterwards Sir Theodore) who had been general manager of the London County Council Tramways, became first general manager of part of the tramway system and from 1936 general manager of road transport. He had a remarkably tetentive memory for statistics and could recite unrehearsed the relevant figures about many LPTB routes. This made him a delightful companion and an ideal person to interview about the Board's activities and as at that time I was dealing with road transport matters for *Modern Transport* I saw quite a lot of him. During his term of office interesting alterations were made to the structure of services in

114

A London General NS type on all-night bus service outside Liverpool Street station early one morning about to depart for Turnham Green.

Central London. The old-established terminus at Elephant & Castle for service 10 and its associates from the direction of Leytonstone, which had been avoided by extension to Pecham Rye as 200 briefly, was bypassed by diversion along Borough Road, Lambeth Bridge and Horseferry Road to Victoria Station and services along York Road and Stamford Street were linked with those via Tooley Street to Greenwich as 70.

Sir Theodore planned a number of other suburban innovations, but as he ruefully told me, a proposal to extend a route which went in the direction of Petts Wood to the station and thence to Orpington drew protests from both Orpington and Bromley, both councils being afraid of trade going to the other. Nowadays service 94 that in his time ran Brockley Rise and Southborough (in the purlieus of Bromley) goes to Orpington and on Monday to Friday peak hours is extended via St Mary Cray to Sidcup station.

Golders Green had a splendid station yard; after the

first world war an extension, intended from as long before as 1902 was opened to Hendon Central which was reached on 19 November 1923 and to Edgware (reached 18 August 1924). At Edgware a bus garage was built and ample facilities for buses were provided there and at Hendon Central.

The reconstruction of the City & South London Railway was carried out in 1924; the link from Euston to Camden Town was opened on 20 April 1924; that from Charing Cross to Kennington was in service on 13 September 1926 and on the same day the extension from Clapham Common to Morden was opened. Simultaneously a series of short routes operated with K-type single-deck buses was begun from Morden to Worcester Park station, to Cheam, to Wallington, to Banstead and to Burgh Heath; at first some of these services were double-deck and started from Charing Cross and others went on circular routes from Morden station to Morden station. The first livery chosen for these K-type single-deckers was in a grey cellulose finish with Johnson style lettering.

An inquiry under the London Traffic Act 1924 into travelling facilities to North and North-East London was held in October 1925 and showed considerable public disquiet about the change from tube to tram or bus at Finsbury Park. The London & North Eastern Railway had plenty of paper plans for the electrification of their suburban services, but it suffered from a chronic shortage of money and when it tried for a loan under the Developments (Loans, Grants and Guarantees) Act it was too late. The inquiry suggested spreading the change over a longer front; the Piccadilly Line was extended (the LNER having waived the right to veto obtained by the Great Northern) to Manor House, where tram and bus exchange platforms were built in the middle of the road, Turnpike Lane (bus terminal facilities), Wood Green (where a sign indicated that an Enfield tram was waiting in Lordship Lane), Bounds Green and Arnos Grove (opened 19 September 1932). The next section was to Southgate and Enfield West (soon renamed Oakwood owing to its distance from Enfield) and was opened on 13 March 1933 and the final portion to Cockfosters on 31 July 1933. As a soured LNER spokesman prophesied, several of these stations rapidly became railheads for connecting bus services and bus and Piccadilly Line through season tickets were issued. A bold stroke was the inauguration of a trolleybus service on 18 October 1936 over an intended tram route from Wood Green station (projected from Winchmore Hill) to Walthamstow and Woodford which proved the traffic possibilities of the Walthamstow area for the Victoria Line tube when that was at last constructed. There was also a trolleybus service from Manor House.

The 1935 plan vastly expanded London Transport; the tubes shot out from the central core over former Great Eastern and Great Northern suburban lines and on separate tracks alongside the Great Western Birmingham line. Unfortunately these schemes were caught unfinished by the second world war and some of the works owing to changed circumstances, such as the imposition of Green Belt restrictions had to be abandoned. The once prosperous Great Northern routes had had minimal train services in wartime, except on the Barnet and Mill Hill East branches and a single-deck bus sufficed for the needs of Alexandra Palace. The Northern Line service to East Finchley began on 3 July 1939 and over the LNER branch to High Barnet on 14 April 1940. Rather as an afterthought the branch as far as Mill Hill East from Finchley Central was brought into service as a single-track on 18 May 1941.

Saddest of all the abandonments was the construction, partly-finished, of a viaduct from Edgware to Brockley Hill and the tube tunnels thence under Stanmore Hill with the Bushey Heath car shed; the latter, because it was used for aircraft construction during the war was sanctioned for industrial use despite its location in the Green Belt and it became first an overhaul works for London Transport buses which at the time were estimated as likely to exceed 12,000 when buses had replaced trams and trolleybuses, and was later used by the Leyland group. This line to Bushey Heath was originally authorised as a railway from Watford to the Great Northern at Edgware in 1897 and was successor to many other schemes; the right-of-way had been safeguarded even to the extent of diverting power lines from the path of the tube extension.

So the former Great Northern lines are derelict from the junction at Finsbury Park to Park Junction and the length of the Alexandra Palace branch and beyond Mill Hill East to Edgware; Mill Hill East is an interchange, although when I went there a couple of years ago I had to wait 30min before I had the pleasure of seeing a bus. The Piccadilly line interchanges at Manor House, Turnpike Lane and Wood Green are well used and Arnos Grove is the starting point of two routes — one to the Barnet neighbourhood and the other cross-country to Edgware station and Stanmore station on the Metropolitan line. Along the Cockfosters line other important stations developed as interchange points are Southgate, Oakwood and Cockfosters itself. The stations on the High Barnet branch are not well placed for the development of feeder bus routes and the theory has been advanced that under the 1935 programme the London Passenger Transport Board would have done better to ignore the Great Northern branch and build a new tube to High Barnet to serve the shopping centres and other points where traffic originates. It is pleasant to think that after many years of lying in abeyance the original concept of Great Northern suburban trains through to the Great Northern & City tube tunnels to Moorgate which were made 16ft diameter for the purpose) has been carried into effect in 1976.

Over the years a much more tolerant attitude is detectable in London Transport traffic staff; at one time they had rigid rules such as counting one person in ten as a potential bus passenger; I remember before the war advocating a certain route (since covered by an independent under licence) and it being turned down flat because of road width. The really remarkable thing is what a good network of services London Transport supplied over the whole metropolis and its least important suburbs.

Like the Back of a Bus

A stern reminder from D. FEREDAY GLENN

DOCKS
9 MILLBROOK
SHIRLEY

The back end of a Southampton Guy Arab III/Park Royal, with spectators watching the Jubilee Naval Review in 1977.

Two trolleybuses, exiled from their native systems at Reading and Glasgow, awaiting transportation to a new home after private preservation. The Reading double-decker is a Sunbeam S7 with Park Royal body, and the single-decker was one of Glasgow's extra-long BUT ETB1s with Burlingham body.

Two classic 1947 Leyland-bodied Titan PD2s of Exeter Corporation at Heavitree Road depot in 1968.

Half an Atlantean at Portsmouth — a Corporation PDR2/1 model with single-deck Pennine 40-seat body.

The austerity look of the 1940s, represented by one of the few utility bodies to escape rebuilding or the scrapyard — the preserved ex-London Transport G351, a 1945 Guy Arab II with Park Royal body.

G 351

I USE **LODGE** PLUGS

WATCH YOUR STEP

C124

'ASPRO' BEATS THE 'FLU

HGC 130

Above: *The yellow and cream livery of Alexanders (Northern) admirably suited the delightful Burlingham body of this 1948 Daimler CVD6.*

Below: *Unmistakably Harrington coachwork, with its dorsal fin, a 1949 AEC Regal III at the 1972 Weymouth Rally.*

Paisley Patterns

Photographs by GAVIN BOOTH

Paisley, with the largest population in Scotland outside the four main cities, has a long tradition of independent bus operation. There are still four independents working in the town, like Graham's, which for many years standardised on Guy Arab double deckers. A line of Guys, bought new and from East Kent, is seen at the Hawkhead garage.

More recently, the Graham's fleet has included Daimler Fleetlines and Leyland Atlanteans. This Alexander-bodied Fleetline is seen in Paisley on the Linwood service.

Paton of Renfrew bought second-hand Leyland double-deckers for many years to maintain its share of the Paisley-Renfrew Ferry service, though in recent years new single-deckers have been favoured. These ex-Edinburgh Corporation all-Leyland Titan PD2/12s (above left) are seen at the Paton garage. In contrast, McGill, Barrhead, has concentrated on new buses, like this low-height Alexander-bodied Daimler Fleetline (above).

An earlier McGill Fleetline, a 1964 model with normal-height Alexander body, seen when new.

A Paisley area independent that is now no more. The services of Smith, Barrhead, controlled by the Scottish Co-operative Wholesale Society, were taken over by Western SMT in 1968. This Leyland Titan PD2 (above left) had a lowbridge Alexander body. Cunningham, Paisley, operates on the service to Renfrew Ferry, and has bought several ex-Ribble Leyland PD3/4s with Burlingham bodies like this one (above).

With Renfrew Ferry on the left, an ex-Northern General Leyland Tiger Cub/Saro sits by the River Clyde in 1967.

With nine countries in the Common Market and a separate European Free Trade area, it would be logical to imagine a few international bus designs, developed by manufacturers to meet common needs.

There is none.

Yet you can travel in Europe and see similar-looking vehicles in different countries, so what has happened?

The answer so far is little. Makers which are export-minded have certainly developed and sold overseas for many years, Leyland and Mercedes being two obvious examples. Neither has yet built a special European bus for the simple reason that there is no standard European bus buyer, and nor is there yet a standard set of construction and use regulations.

Leyland made a brave attempt to meet almost all known regulations in most parts of the world with the Leyland National, yet it hasn't sold well in Europe, not even in a Leyland stronghold like Holland.

The Dutch have their own ideas about city buses when it comes to things like windscreens (they are keen on anti-dazzle designs which use multi-piece flat glasses set at angles which instead create blind spots at the joints) and doors (three doorways, the last very near the back of the bus, where the floor height is excessive on rear-engined designs) or roof hatches (in case the bus plunges into a canal, roof hatches have to be fully opening for passengers to leave that way).

The French, the Germans, the Swedes, the Italians and many others, all have their own ideas — happily for the enthusiast at least. There is no dominating chassis builder, no international bodybuilder.

At the moment many of the makers are busy trying to get a foothold in another country or two, a process

The European Bus: Myth or Reality?

Now that the European nations have forged closer links with each other, has this new unity spread to bus design, asks JOHN ALDRIDGE, as he takes a Cook's tour looking for common designs.

that some began a long time ago.

Sometimes the results are not too clever. Make A can be so busy wooing country X that it finds foreign make B has meanwhile got in with one of its own customers. For every successful first-time sale — conquest sales they are sometimes called — somebody else somewhere must lose, unless a maker goes out of business. Then there can be big opportunities. But most surviving European chassis-makers are probably too well entrenched in cars or trucks as well to be likely to drop out. Berliet, Saviem and Renault is one of the last groupings to be completed. Only Italy looks a little vulnerable with, last time I counted, 17 different bodybuilders.

For the chassis builder in particular there are two ways to build up trade. He can woo a handful of large potential customers in a few countries or, like Volvo, he can deliberately aim to sell only a modest number of bus and coach chassis in many markets. Volvo is happy with — indeed prefers — 50 or maybe 100 bus and coach chassis sales a year in a particular country because it is less vulnerable to competitors or to the effects of financial cutbacks in individual countries.

Of course, it isn't as easy as that. The climate or the operating conditions in Italy are not like those in Finland and a chassis that works well in one place may not be reliable in another. And different operators in different places expect — or are used to — varying standards of reliability.

In Spring 1977 I was in Madrid, for a couple of days and surprised by what I saw. There were rear-engined Pegaso single-deckers expiring in clouds of steam at a rate which would make any British rear-engined chassis designer feel quite superior. At some busy bus city centre stops there were water hoses permanently available, suggesting that the problem — whether it be maintenance or design — was not a new one.

So if there is no European design or designs yet, it is more fun to take a general look at some of the countries. This is not an exhaustive survey and covers only most of Western Europe — you would have to be a very wealthy enthusiast even to keep tabs on what was happening in each capital city.

Germany with makers Mercedes, Magirus Deutz, Setra and MAN is an obvious starting place. Ten years ago, the municipal operators got their standardised bus design off the ground. It is named after the municipal association, the Verband Offentlicher Verkehrsbetriebe, and known as the VöV You can find Büssings (now part of MAN) of this design in Hamburg, or Mercedes there too or in Kiel or Dusseldorf or dozens of other places...

But don't go thinking they are all the same. Each chassis has, of course, its own make of engine and main components but there have been a number of changes to or departures from the — to British eyes — rigid specifications. Length was originally set at 11 metres (36ft 1in) but some of the Hamburg Büssings are 9.4 metres (30ft 9in) and others are

Opposite: *ITALY — A one-man operated Lancia with three-door OMS body in suburban Milan.*

HOLLAND — Outwardly like Daf standard city buses, this Rotterdam vehicle boasts a Leyland Panther chassis.

11.3 metres (37ft) long . . .

Surprisingly, for a rear-engined city bus, they started off with synchromesh gearboxes and not automatic. The orginal ugly sharply curved windscreen has changed to one more like the familiar BET screen. And if you looked at a 1974 MAN you would find the rationalised D.25 series engine with many parts interchangeable with the truck engines had the cylinder heads lying on the left, whereas the earlier MAN VöV bus had the heads on the right . . .

But all this is not to detract on what is an outstanding effort, the results of which can be found not only in Germany, where the Mercedes 0.305 is the best-known example, but elsewhere in Europe and in Australia and New Zealand and South Africa. You can also find Mercedes 0.305s, virtually to VoV standard, but with Heuliez bodies, in France in a number of places.

Over now to Holland for another standard bus, with an even more rigid specification. Originally known as the Three Cities bus, it can now be found in five Dutch cities and across the border as well. In the mid-1960s Amsterdam, the Hague and Rotterdam all got together to design a standard vehicle which was even painted the same colour irrespective of operator. The original prototypes were on Leyland Panther and Daf chassis. Over 1,000 on Daf chassis have since been built, plus one on a rear-engined Volvo B59. The project owed much to the enthusiasm — and determination — of a few individuals in the three undertakings, something that was not found when two of them built underground railways subsequently — the rolling stock is different!

Holland is also the home of another large rationalised fleet, that of the 'daughter' companies of the State Railways. Leyland Worldmasters are popular here, as are Daf chassis and more recently, integral vehicles built by bodybuilder Den Oudsten.

Above left: *SWITZERLAND — A four-door Hess-bodied FBW articulated trolleybus in service in Geneva early in 1978.*

Right: *ITALY — The bizarre back end of a prototype Viberti double-decker built for Turin — very clearly a rear-engined design.*

Left: *ITALY — Trams and buses share a roadway in Turin; the bus is a Viberti-bodied Fiat with Paris-style under-the-driver engine.*

Above: *FRANCE* — The Parisienne suburb of Chelles has its own small — and varied — orange-liveried fleet. It includes Spanish-built Pegaso 6050s like this one.

Right: *DENMARK* — A Volvo B59 in the Copenhagen municipal fleet; more recent deliveries have been built by DAB, a Leyland subsidiary.

All are overhauled at a big works at Utrecht: liveries used to be different, but now all are the standard yellow, Government inspired, which has appeared everywhere in Holland other than on city buses. City buses are dark red and grey. It was government inspiration of a different kind, in a different age, that led to the rather drab green until recently to be found on every Italian city bus. Mussolini decreed it in the 1930s and it remained until the 1970s. When I visited the Fiat bodybuilding plant a few years ago, they were still put out about the different colours different cities were now painting their buses... Turin in red and cream, Milan in orange, Rome in green, Bologna in ... it was all most inconvenient.

Italy is also a country for standardised city buses, its operators' association being the Federazione Nazionale Trasporti Pubblici Enti Locali, Federtran for short. Its bus, built by Fiat of course, comes in 11- and 12-metre lengths, the longer being four doored, with two paired doorways in the middle. Some operators, Rome for example, have both sizes in the fleet.

All have the same strange-looking low chassis, with flat engine under the driver (Paris style) and rather low ground clearance, with single tyres all round. The chassis is not self-supporting, so those not being bodied by Fiat can be seen languishing or lolling on transporter lorries en route to the bodybuilder.

Italy is a country of contrasts and you can see these vast buses being one-man operated while round the corner or in the next town there are 20-seater midi-buses still crew-operated.

Mention buses with engines under the driver and think of Paris, the largest operator of the design, though such vehicles can be found elsewhere in France. One of the latest Parisienne ideas is a revival of a previous one, the open rear platform. The new ones, and some conversions, can be found on routes popular with tourists, though the platform can only be approached from inside the vehicle. You don't enter and leave that way like you used to.

But not all Paris buses have the engine under the driver. The RATP is at present evaluating various foreign makes as, incidentally, is the Brussels

undertaking. And Paris has a batch of rear-engined Berliet PR 100s with rather strikingly-styled bodies, on an outer suburban service to Orly. Similar vehicles, with throaty Perkins V8 engines, can be found in a plain all-cream livery in the Monte Carlo fleet. And in the Paris suburb of Chelles, served also by RATP, you can find in the small municipal fleet a splendid assortment of Mercedes, Setra and Pegaso vehicles, all painted a striking orange.

Switzerland is worth a study tour of its own. Local makes build to a very high quality, giving exceptionally long life, but the price has not pleased all potential customers and production has not always kept pace with demand. As a result even the PTT post bus network runs some Mercedes, and in the cities, there are Volvos as well as Danish-built DABs. The DABs have Leyland engines (DAB is a Leyland subsidiary) or Saurer engines.

And if you go to Denmark, to Copenhagen, you can find B59 Volvos and DABs.

Other countries woorthy of a mention are Spain, of course, with mainly Pegaso city buses — the company is state-owned: Leyland used to have a big shareholding — and also some by Barreiros (a Chrysler subsidiary) and Portugal with its AEC double-deckers in Lisbon, and locally-assembled AECs common generally. Lisbon also boasts probably the last half-cab single-decker bodies to be built: they appeared in the early 1970s, on older AEC Regal chassis.

Then there is Sweden with, naturally, Scanias (making the same sounds as Metropolitan double-deckers in Britain) and Volvos, some with Hungarian-built Ikarus bodies. Articulated buses have become popular in Swedish cities, and in Switzerland too, and are not uncommon in Germany or Spain. The front half is usually of underfloor-engine layout because the rear-engined chassis would have too high a floor level. But there are at least two designs with powered pusher units now undergoing trials. Interest in artics generally seems to be growing.

In short then, no matter where you go in Europe there should be plenty of bus interest. And if you go to more than one country there might be a design you think you've seen before. If Barcelona's older buses look familiar, for example, it's because some Pegasos were based on Italian Viberti designs which could be found, for example, in Turin.